ICETE Series

Excellence in Theological Education

Global Hub for Evangelical Theological Education

GLOBAL LIBRARY

Many of us in Asia became involved in leadership in theological education right after obtaining our doctoral degrees; often without professional training in governance, administration, curriculum . . . the list goes on. We draw from Dr Steve Hardy's long years of experience. This practical book is an excellent guide for Asian theological educators to help us to achieve excellence in our theological education.

Chiu Eng Tan, PhD
Academic Dean, Biblical Seminary of the Philippines

Dr Steve Hardy shares his vast experience of three decades as a theological educator, drawing on visits to more than one hundred theological training institutions throughout the non-Western world. His insights are not only theoretical, but are rooted and linked with praxis through his own teaching, seminars, and through leaders he has mentored.

Sebastiao Lucio Guimaraes, PhD
Former Director, Evangelical Missions Training Center, Vicosa, MG Brazil

I consider Steve Hardy´s book a very practical guide for leaders of theological schools. For us, it´s been helpful on our training seminars at various levels. He provides a map of the most important aspects that institutions of theological education should consider to accomplish their task successfully. He also includes valuable insights to deal with the challenges common in contexts of limited resources and some of the standards to measure up excellence in what we do.

Oscar Campos, PhD
Director, Seminario Teologico Centro-Americano (SETECA), Guatemala

"Excellence or mediocrity" is the key challenge for present-day theological education as theological schools mushroom in the Majority World. Dr Hardy challenges and provides holistic and practical insights for theological education from his vast experience. This book is a must read for all involved in theological education to move from good to excellence in our endeavor.

Ashish Chrispal, PhD
Regional Director, Overseas Council Asia,
Former Principal, South Asia Institute of Advanced Christian Studies (SAIACS), Bangalore, India

Whether you are principal, dean, board member or another position of high responsibility in theological institutions, you will be significantly encouraged and helped by this book.

Paul Sanders, PhD
Former International Director (and Academic Dean),
Arab Baptist Seminary, Beirut, Lebanon
Former Director, International Council for Evangelical
Theological Education (ICETE)

Excellence in Theological Education

Effective Training for Church Leaders

Steven A. Hardy

GLOBAL LIBRARY

© 2016 by Steven A. Hardy

Published 2016 by Langham Global Library
An imprint of Langham Publishing
www.langhampublishing.org

Langham Publishing and its imprints are a ministry of Langham Partnership

Langham Partnership
PO Box 296, Carlisle, Cumbria CA3 9WZ, UK
www.langham.org

First published in 2006 by Booksurge, distributed in Africa by SIM and distributed in Asia by LBCS Publishing Unit.

This edition published 2016 by Langham Global Library.

ISBNs:
978-1-78368-202-7 Print
978-1-78368-203-4 ePub
978-1-78368-205-8 PDF

Steven A. Hardy has asserted his right under the Copyright, Designs and Patents Act, 1988 to be identified as the Author of this work.

All rights reserved. No part of this publication may be reproduced, stored in a retrieval system or transmitted, in any form or by any means, electronic, mechanical, photocopying, recording or otherwise, without the prior written permission of the publisher or the Copyright Licensing Agency.

All Scripture quotations, unless otherwise indicated, are taken from the Holy Bible, New International Version®, NIV®. Copyright © 1973, 1978, 1984 by Biblica, Inc.™ Used by permission of Zondervan.

British Library Cataloguing in Publication Data
A catalogue record for this book is available from the British Library

ISBN: 978-1-78368-202-7

Cover & Book Design: projectluz.com

Langham Partnership actively supports theological dialogue and an author's right to publish but does not necessarily endorse the views and opinions set forth, and works referenced within this publication or guarantee its technical and grammatical correctness. Langham Partnership does not accept any responsibility or liability to persons or property as a consequence of the reading, use or interpretation of its published content.

Contents

	Preface	xi
1	What Is Excellence?	1
	Is Excellence Biblical?	1
	Is Excellence Being (or Having Been) the Best of the Bunch?	3
	Is Excellence Equal to Success?	5
	Is Excellence a Relative Thing?	6
	Who Determines the Standards or Affirms One's Excellence?	7
	Is Excellence Possible?	10
	Conclusions	10
	Discussion Questions Regarding Excellence	11
2	Excellence in Leadership	13
	What Is Leadership?	14
	Biblical Concepts of Leadership	15
	Character: Who a Leader Needs to Be	18
	Responsibilities: What a Leader Needs to Do	20
	Discovering and Developing Leadership	22
	Styles and Varieties of Leadership	23
	Working Together as a Team	24
	Resolving Tensions and Conflict	26
	Negotiating Leadership Transition	27
	Conclusions	28
	Discussion Questions Regarding Your Leadership	28
	Suggestions for Further Reading	29
3	Excellence in Strategic Planning	33
	What Strategic Planning Is Not	34
	Developing a Strategic Plan	37
	And If You Don't Have a Strategic Plan: Write One!	48
	Conclusions	49
	Discussion Questions Regarding Your Strategic Plan	49
	Suggestions for Further Reading	50
4	Excellence in Governance	51
	Are Boards Worth the Effort?	51
	Whose Theological Training Program or Institution Is It?	53

	The Role of Ownership in Governance	55
	The General Assembly as an Advisory Board or Advisory Council	56
	The Governing Board	57
	Specific Responsibilities of the Board	61
	Specific Responsibilities of Board Members	62
	The Administrative or Management Team	63
	The Governance Role of the Principal	64
	Conclusions	65
	Discussion Questions Regarding Your Governance	65
	Suggestions for Further Reading	66
5	**Excellence in Administration**	**67**
	The Challenge of Administration	68
	Appropriate Administrative Structures	70
	Developing a Budget	75
	How Much Administrative Staff Is Too Much?	76
	Caution: Don't take on unnecessary administration!	77
	Job Descriptions	78
	Hiring New People	79
	Strengthening the Administrative Staff Team That We Have	81
	Conclusions	82
	Discussion Questions Regarding Your Administration	82
	Suggestions for Further Reading	83
6	**Excellence in Curriculum**	**85**
	What Is Curriculum?	86
	God's Curricular Plan	88
	What Curriculum Is Fundamentally Not	90
	How People Learn	91
	What a Curricular Plan Needs to Be	93
	Three Basic Types of Curriculum	96
	Character Development	97
	Course Design	99
	A Syllabus Needs to Include:	100
	Using Curricular Materials	101
	Writing Your Own Curricular Materials	102
	Conclusions	102
	Discussion Questions Regarding Your Curriculum	103
	Suggestions for Further Reading	103

7	Excellence in Teachers............................... 105
	Factors in Developing the Faculty That We Need 106
	Caring for the Teachers That We Have 110
	Finding New Teachers 112
	Formal Faculty Development – Advanced Study 115
	One Advantage of Investing in Your Teachers 118
	Conclusions 119
	Discussion Questions Regarding Your Teachers 119
	Suggestions for Further Reading 120
8	Excellence in Facilities............................... 121
	Using Your Space Effectively 122
	Site Plans 122
	Maintenance Plans and Budgets 123
	What Image Are You Trying to Give? 124
	Appropriate Building Projects 124
	Well-designed Building Projects 125
	Funding Your Building Projects 126
	Conclusions 127
	Discussion Questions Regarding Your Facilities 127
9	Excellence in Libraries............................... 129
	What Is a Library? 130
	Building the Library Collection 131
	Library Facilities 134
	Library Personnel 136
	How to Help Those Who Don't (or Won't) Have Easy Access to a Library 137
	Conclusions 138
	Discussion Questions Regarding Your Library 138
	Website Suggestions for Further Study 138
	Suggestions for Further Reading 139
10	Excellence in Fundraising............................ 141
	Why Do We Struggle to Have Enough? 142
	Developing a Fundraising Strategy 145
	Financial Support from Relationships 150
	Conclusions 156
	Discussion Questions Regarding Your Fundraising .. 157
	Websites on Grantmaking, Fundraising and Foundations ... 157

    Suggestions for Further Reading ... 157
    Appendix to Chapter 10: Writing Project Proposals ... 159

11 Excellence in Extending Training ... 161
    Distance or Extension Training ... 162
    Extending Ourselves by Serving Our Graduates ... 163
    Extending Ourselves by Serving Other Training Institutions ... 165
    Extending Ourselves by Serving Churches and the Community ... 168
    Extending Ourselves Formally ... 170
    Why Extension Education May Fail ... 175
    Conclusions ... 175
    Discussion Questions Regarding the Extension of Your Training ... 176
    Websites concerning Electronic Distance Education ... 177
    Suggestions for Further Reading ... 177

12 Excellence in Evaluation and Renewal ... 179
    Is It Worth the Time and Expense? ... 180
    Organizational Life Cycles ... 181
    The Renewal of Your Training ... 182
    The Renewal of Your People: Why? ... 184
    The Renewal of Your People: How? ... 186
    Becoming a Learning Community ... 188
    Conclusions ... 192
    Discussions Questions Regarding Your Evaluation and Renewal ... 192
    Suggestions for Further Reading ... 193

Preface

This book is designed to help theological school leadership, especially within the non-Western world, to affirm the excellence of their training institutions, and where excellence may be lacking, to discover ideas that will strengthen the quality of what they have.

It has been said that when you look behind a successful young man, someone who is making a difference in the lives of others, you will find a fairly astonished mother-in-law. But I suspect that you won't find astonished teachers. What a privilege for a teacher to be involved in the lives of those that God has gifted and called for his service. I love the impact that training has on multiplying and strengthening the mission and work of the church. Over the years, it has been satisfying to watch my students move beyond their teacher in skills and effectively go places that I could never have gone.

I grew up with parents as teachers, and have "played school" for most of my adult life. I first discovered non-formal education in the early 1970s through inductive Bible studies. My paradigms of leadership were permanently scrambled in the dark days of Ethiopia in the mid-1970s as I watched God use people with no formal training whatsoever. During six years in West-Central Brazil, I discovered how truly ignorant I was about all things educational as I helped open a new seminary, including writing curricula and doing teacher training. But we learned a lot about modeling. We had no funding, so all our teachers were full-time practitioners, sharing their experience and wisdom with our students. In Brazil, I also was involved in church planting and in church-based evening extension programs using programmed textbooks.

In 1985 our family moved to Mozambique to prepare leadership for a church that had grown phenomenally during the communist days. I reopened a little seminary and prepared teaching materials, training young leaders to be teachers in a countrywide program of theological education by extension.

In the 1990s I visited over one hundred seminaries and Bible schools throughout Africa and elsewhere as the theological education advisor for the Africa Evangelical Fellowship (now SIM), and as an occasional consultant to other Christian organizations. I listened to the many needs and concerns while being impressed with the quality of those who give leadership to leadership training programs. Many of these have (like me) stepped into educational administrative roles with little or no preparation for those responsibilities so perhaps it wasn't surprising to note how many of these leaders were on the edge of exhaustion.

In 1998 I become the director of Overseas Council International's Theological Resource Team. One satisfying part of that job was developing and directing the Institute for Excellence in Global Theological Education. The "Institute" was designed to hone the skills of theological school leaders in areas of educational administration. Although OCI considered most of its partner programs to be excellent, many of the leaders of these programs lived in isolation from other training programs and honestly had little idea how their programs compared to anything other than the institution in which they themselves had studied.

As a donor organization, OCI wanted to invest in projects that grew out of strategic planning, and to partner with training institutions that were willing to invest in their own leadership. For our sake and for theirs, we wanted to know if our partner programs knew how to put together a comprehensive strategic plan. Did their plan include practical ways to develop and care for a quality teaching and administrative leadership team? Did they have a plan for strengthening a curriculum that equipped quality students for effective ministry? Were they building good relations with their constituency to find adequate resources to finance the training program?

The Institute was designed as a five-day forum where school leadership could discuss issues like these. Not only did we want to help the leaders of our partner programs acquire or renew the tools they needed for being quality training institutions, we also wanted to create a network and environment in which leaders could encourage one another.

Part of the reason that I use the word "excellence" in this book is my admiration for the impact of OCI's Institute for Excellence. However, for some, "excellence" is a buzzword more associated with the business community than with the world of education. It connotes efficiency and productivity while the reality is that training those God has called to be leaders is not always cost-effective or efficient. Our own personal stories are illustrations of how God has led and equipped each of us through a wide variety of unique experiences throughout our lifetimes. So how can we affirm "excellence" when each and every student is also gifted uniquely and comes with unique experiences?

As I will discuss in chapter 1 of this book, excellence is a biblical concept and one that is valid educationally, although it must be seen within a context. I identify key areas in which excellence is needed in order for a training institution to affirm its own excellence. Each of these areas forms one chapter in this book. We will look at:

Excellence in Leadership (chapter 2)

An excellent leadership training institution understands what leadership is and how it can be encouraged, trained and used. Good programs know how to take advantage of differing styles of leaders. Finding, encouraging and developing good leaders may be the most important piece of what makes a good program excellent.

Excellence in Strategic Planning (chapter 3)

Without a clear idea of where one is going, it is difficult to know whether or not anything is being accomplished. An excellent leadership training institution takes the time to develop and routinely review a strategic plan that includes discovering its values, defining its mission in the light of needs, assessing its own strengths and weaknesses and then prayerfully dreaming in order to develop a doable plan that takes it to where it ought to go.

Excellence in Governance (chapter 4)

Excellent leadership training institutions are accountable to the constituencies that they serve. They are advised and governed by well-conceived and supportive advisory councils and governing boards.

Excellence in Administration (chapter 5)

Excellent leadership training institutions have appropriate and adequate structures that make the program work well. Good administration is done by people who have clear job descriptions and who are competent and willing to serve the teachers, staff and students so that learning occurs.

Excellence in Curriculum (chapter 6)

There is no perfect curriculum where "one size fits all." An excellent training program equips specific students for ministry within a specific context. Its curriculum is creatively taught by teachers whose lives illustrate what they are saying.

Excellence in Teachers (chapter 7)
The most important single resource that a program has is its teaching team. Excellent training institutions know how to find, train and encourage their teachers.

Excellence in Facilities (chapter 8)
Excellent training institutions have adequate academic, administrative and research facilities that are maintained properly.

Excellence in Libraries (chapter 9)
An excellent library is systematically collected according to a selection policy built on the mission statement of the library and of the school. Trained personnel organize it for maximum usefulness to both students and faculty. The excellent libraries of the future will not be built on printed materials alone, but will take full advantage of information available globally through information technology.

Excellence in Fundraising (chapter 10)
An excellent leadership training institution is adequately funded to do what the strategic plan says should be done. It takes responsibility for its financial health and builds self-reliance. An excellent program maintains good relationships with its friends, churches and ministries, and especially with its students once they graduate. It benefits from healthy partnerships, especially with those who claim it as their training program.

Excellence in Extending Your Training (chapter 11)
Excellent training institutions extend their influence and training beyond their campuses. They serve their graduates and the ministries and communities of their graduates in a variety of formal and non-formal ways. They make good use of information technology, both on campus and in their extension efforts.

Excellence in Evaluation and Renewal (chapter 12)
Organizational transformation and renewal is present at each stage in the life of an excellent training institution. Evaluation is structured into the ongoing

life of each aspect of the program. Being a part of a broader network and learning from others is an important part of renewal.

You undoubtedly will note that few of these thoughts are original with me. What I have tried to write is what I hopefully would share while sitting in the office of a friend who is in a position of leadership in a Bible school or seminary. These words are not primarily written for your specialized staff – such as your librarian, financial manager or the IT guru. My concern is for those who give leadership to a school's entire program. What do *you* need to be, to know, or to know how to do in order to promote excellence in all areas of your institution? My prayer is that you will find encouragement and useful advice as you affirm your own excellence and as you work to strengthen and build quality into what you already have.

This is not a research paper, so I have kept reference notes to a minimum, but where they seem appropriate, I include them in the text. Some of the more important books, articles and electronic links on each subject are listed at the end of each chapter. Questions at the end of each chapter will help you and your leadership team to evaluate your own training program.

I owe special thanks to those who were my friends, colleagues and mentors at OCI, especially John Bennett, Jack Graves, Manfred Kohl and Stefanii Morton Ferenczi. Thanks also to several colleagues working in different areas of the non-Western world who have given me feedback on this manuscript: Vera Brock (Brazil), Lee Christenson (USA), Scott Cunningham (Nigeria), Fritz Deininger (Thailand), Bill Houston (South Africa), Steve Parr (Canada), Paul Sanders (Lebanon), Chuck Saunders (South Africa) and Rich Starcher (Kenya). My deepest debt, however, is to my wife, LeAnne, who not only risked our marital happiness as she carefully edited the details of this book, but who has for years been gently (and not so gently) pushing me to finally get this written! And thanks be to God, in whom and for whom we exist.

If you have comments or suggestions, or if you would be interested in talking further about any of the issues discussed in this book, please feel free to contact the author at steve.hardy@sim.org.

1

What Is Excellence?

According to the *Merriam-Webster Online* dictionary, "excellent" means very good, first class, superior. As a quality, the dictionary suggests that excellence implies virtue or something that is valuable. So it would seem that if our theological education institutions can demonstrate quality and values, our public relations brochures should be able to declare that we are first class, superior and excellent. We are more than just "adequate," we are very good at doing what we do.

Evangelical leadership training programs are strategic places where present and future leaders are equipped for work within the kingdom of God. Leaders of leadership training programs should be able to affirm the extent to which their programs are quality institutions. However, how can we recognize or acknowledge excellence, given the wide variety of training programs doing good things differently, especially in the light of the almost endless ways in which we know that our own training institutions could be better? In this chapter we would like to examine how we can understand the term "excellent." Is this only a public relations "buzz word" borrowed from the popular literature of the business community? Or are there both biblical and educational foundations to the concept of being first-rate? To what extent is excellence related to perfection, success or just being the best of the bunch? Who affirms our excellence or decides what standards we are to live up to? And is excellence even possible?

Is Excellence Biblical?

The Lord does the right things in the right way. In Genesis 1 we read that he gazed on the creation with satisfaction. God had done exactly what he intended to do, by the power of his word. He liked what he saw and affirmed, "It is good!" We recognize incomparable quality in character, in results and in process. Excellence is seen in who God is, in what he does and in how he does it.

God is at work in the world around us and in us. The day is yet to come when we will be changed in the twinkling of an eye (1 Cor 15:51), though even now Paul can say: "It is God who works in you, to will and to act according to his good purpose" (Phil 2:13). "In all things God works for the good of those who love him, who have been called according to his purpose" (Rom 8:28). As we note chaos and confusion around us, it is reassuring to know that God has a plan and that everything works according to that plan. In the end, "all things in heaven and on earth [will be brought] together under one head, even Christ" (Eph 1:10). We are being renewed and transformed by the living God to his glory and to achieve his purposes. All of God's ways are perfect and his excellent plans will succeed. In a song written for public worship, the Psalmist wrote, "O Lord, our Lord, how majestic is your name in all the earth!" (Ps 8:1). To borrow the language of the business world, the benchmarks or standards of excellence are clear in God's character. The best practices of what should be done, and how, are visible in all the works of God.

However, God alone is perfect and holy in all his ways. We cannot do what God does. There is no one like God. This is understood among Amish women, who are known for the high-quality quilts that they make. Yet these women intentionally put a flaw in their otherwise perfect quilts as a way of humbly acknowledging that only God is perfect. In this sense, excellence, like holiness, is something that we can only appreciate as we look at ultimate standards, way beyond what we could ever expect to attain. We all fall short of the glory of God (Rom 3:23). It is not possible to have a school with "zero defects."

Nevertheless, learning to appreciate excellence is something that we are encouraged to do. The Apostle Paul said that we are to reflect on that which is excellent. To the Philippian church, he wrote: "Finally, brothers, whatever is true, whatever is noble, whatever is right, whatever is pure, whatever is lovely, whatever is admirable – if anything is *excellent* or praiseworthy – think about such things" (Phil 4:8).[1]

---

1. Italics in Bible quotations have been added by the author.

When Paul wrote to Titus, he indicated that when the church was doing that which was good and profitable for everyone, this was something that could be called *excellent*: "This is a trustworthy saying. And I want you to stress these things, so that those who have trusted in God may be careful to devote themselves to doing what is good. These things are *excellent* and profitable for everyone" (Titus 3:8). Paul says something similar when he describes the value of love, calling this "the most *excellent* way" (1 Cor 12:31).

Excellence is related to the word "excel." So Paul encouraged a church that was good at many things to do even more: "But just as you excel in everything – in faith, in speech, in knowledge, in complete earnestness and in your love for us – see that you also *excel* in this grace of giving" (2 Cor 8:7). In the same way, Paul urged the Thessalonians to excel: "Finally, brothers, we instructed you how to live in order to please God, as in fact you are living. Now we ask you and urge you in the Lord Jesus to do this more and more" (1 Thess 4:1).

Is Excellence Being (or Having Been) the Best of the Bunch?

In reality, most people (or organizations) tend to feel that they are the best of the bunch. Peters and Waterman present a psychological study done with a random sample of male adults.[2] When asked to rank themselves on their ability to get along with other people, "*all* subjects, 100%, put themselves in the top half of the population. 60% rated themselves in the top 10% percent of the population and a full 25% ever so humbly thought they were in the top 1% of the population." In a parallel finding, "70% rated themselves in the top quartile in leadership, [while] only 2% felt they were below average as leaders." As it related to athletic ability, "60% said they were in the top quartile" with only 6% feeling that they were "below average." It's not bad for people to have positive views of themselves. However, given a rather common tendency to evaluate ourselves unrealistically, self-assessment alone can neither establish our excellence, nor our lack of it. We need somebody or something to which we can compare ourselves before we can really crow about our superiority. We aren't excellent simply because we say that we are.

---

2. Thomas J. Peters and Robert H. Waterman, *In Search of Excellence* (New York, NY: Warner Books, 1982), 56–57.

Many people and their organizations think that they are tops, even when they are not. College or seminary brochures functionally declare: "We are the greatest! We are excellent! There is no one like us." I once did a paper evaluation of a leadership training program in West Africa. It had less than fifteen students, yet it viewed itself as being *the* premier training program for all of Africa. Their documents (presented in a well-designed color brochure as part of a request for massive funding from the West) suggested world-level impact. It may have been great public relations, but the reality was that this was not a program that was accredited by anyone I knew, and it was totally unknown by anyone I ever met! Their affirmation of excellence was based on nothing other than the high view that they (alone) held of themselves. To truly affirm our excellence, we need objective standards or points of reference against which we can compare ourselves. We aren't excellent simply because we are the only program we know something about.

There are training institutions that have had a history and a reputation for being excellent. Muhammad Ali repeatedly claimed: "I am the greatest!" Even if this was true during the short time that he was the heavyweight boxing champion of the world, it no longer is true today. At best, he *was* the greatest. The leadership of a training program may not realize that they are no longer functioning at a level of quality that existed in earlier days. Such programs may be responding to needs that no longer exist. They may have failed to adopt new methodologies or educational tools that would have helped them to teach better. We aren't excellent simply because we once were.

On the other hand, a leadership training institution may come to the conclusion that it is woefully far from excellent. They see many complicated problems as they evaluate themselves. They feel discouraged, as they don't sense that they are making much of an impact. It may be that their self-understanding is true. However, it also may be that they are unaware of how God is using them in extraordinary ways. Not only are they failing to hear the right feedback, they may be requiring standards of themselves that are unrealistically high. Being good in who we are, in what we do and in how we do it, is something that is best affirmed by others, especially by those who benefit from the program. We aren't far from excellence simply because we feel discouraged.

Is Excellence Equal to Success?

In a sense the answer is yes. God accomplished what he intended to accomplish. That's first-rate. There is excellence or quality when the right things are done in the right ways. But the point is not simply to achieve a goal: it is to achieve the right goals.

Some "successes" are anything but excellent. A drug lord may be successful in cornering the market for selling illegal drugs in a particular city. A person may succeed in becoming rich, yet do so unethically or at the expense of family, relationships or health. Being first-rate involves quality of character and right processes, as well as having the right objectives.

When excellence is fundamentally determined by "success" there is a strong temptation to tell stories that don't exactly present the whole picture. We worked in Brazil between 1977 and 1984. The denomination with which we worked reported baptizing thousands of new believers each year. This "success" should have resulted in wonderful church growth. Yet the statistics of the denomination's annual report showed that each year the total membership of the denomination remained about the same. So while it was good to evangelize and baptize new people, the reality was that each year the denomination was losing as many people as it gained. That's hardly excellence in building a healthy church.

The twenty-first-century edition of *Operation World* (WEC, 2001), states that 91.7 percent of the population of Latin America could be classified as "Christian." Isn't this a success story of effective evangelization? But what then of the syncretism that is present across much of Latin America? This confused mix of beliefs suggests that a much smaller number of people may actually be healthy "born-again believers." In similar ways, statistics would suggest success in the growth of the gospel within the United States. Gallop polls have shown that more than half of the American population calls itself "born again." However, these same polls indicate that there is functionally no difference in values and life style between these "believers" and the general population of the country. If being a "believer" doesn't result in a difference in values or lifestyle, one cannot affirm excellence in the evangelism that was done.

Leadership training institutions can play similar games with the statistics that they share with others. We are not excellent if we are counting the wrong things or simply not counting enough. A training program may successfully have reached its goal of a 50 percent increase in student enrollment over a three-year period. However, were all the new students quality students? And even if they were, does the school now have the capacity to adequately house and feed them? Does it have books, space and teachers to help them learn? Successfully meeting any one particular goal may not necessarily indicate overall excellence in the leadership training program.

A leadership training program may report that its income is up by 20 percent. That may be wonderful, but is it the whole story? For if student enrollment is up by 30 percent, and if new staff members have been hired for the new students, expenses may actually be up by over 50 percent. So in reality the program is worse off than before. Or perhaps the rise in income has come from a large gift from a single overseas donor, with the result that local supporters have concluded that the program no longer needs any help from them. While last year's bills have been paid, in reality the program is in deep financial trouble despite its temporary success. There's not much excellence in these partial stories.

If a training institution reports that all its students successfully passed their exams, that may be worth celebrating. But what exactly was tested in those exams? Can the students preach? Or are they brilliant preachers, but so arrogant that no one wants them as pastors? A program may be successful in bringing every student to graduation, but if they've been trained in the wrong things so that they can't minister effectively, there's not much excellence in the program.

Excellence is more than just a list of "successes," especially if our successes come from bad goals, selective reporting, incomplete analysis or a poor use of statistics. Nevertheless, when we are able to accomplish the right things in the right ways, there is much to rejoice over from our success. The rest of this book is designed to help you discover and celebrate the ways in which you are excellent (or could be excellent) in doing what God intended for you to do.

Is Excellence a Relative Thing?

Yes and no. We assess our quality as we measure ourselves against specific standards and objectives. That's not relative. Yet as we will note shortly, many standards are different for different people and contexts and at different times.

As the purpose or goals of an activity or organization change, so also do the criteria by which we can assess excellence. A graduate level course on marriage counseling should be assessed differently than a seminar offered on a weekend to help married couples know how to communicate better. And both of these will have different standards or criteria of excellence than a sports camp to help young people learn to play football better.

Assessing excellence also depends on the abilities and experience of participants. What one expects from a child just learning to play the piano is different from an adult who has a degree in music. We have different standards of excellence for a beginning preaching student than we do for a homiletics professor. The expectations we have for a new Bible school student learning to reflect on ministry will be different from our expectations for a veteran missionary returning from the field to begin a master's-level program in missiology. The work of both can be excellent, though the output of one will be very different from the other. We affirm excellence to the extent that we have been successful in reaching a standard or goal that is appropriate to the program and to the level of skills and experience of those who participate in that program.

Furthermore, we can affirm excellence in process as one moves or progresses toward values, standards or goals. Not only can excellent progress be made as a person grows or matures, but we also can affirm excellence in the way in which growth is being encouraged. In all of these examples, there is a relative aspect to excellence. Something is being measured or evaluated in specific people with unique gifts and abilities at specific times and in specific contexts – all against values, standards or goals that are appropriate to those being evaluated.

Who Determines the Standards or Affirms One's Excellence?

1. God Himself

Evangelical training programs exist to glorify God. Our individual and institutional desire must be to hear God say, "Well done, good and faithful servant." We have clear standards from God in his Holy Word concerning the training mandate that has been given to us, along with many examples of how training can and should be done. As we attempt to do the task that has been given to us, we need to heed God's Word and to hear God's Spirit in order to walk and work with wisdom. While a final evaluation of our work will only occur at the end of time, when all things will be revealed, God is able to encourage (and correct) us in what we are doing now. May we not be so busy, or so blind and deaf, that we are unable to sense God's presence among us or to hear his voice. May we rejoice and be satisfied in what God has done as we see or hear stories about the lives and ministries of our graduates. And may we be renewed and affirmed by God's Spirit who lives and works in and through us.

2. The Constituent Community

Beyond God himself, the most important place from which we should hear words of affirmation concerning our excellence is the community that we are trying to serve. Feedback from our constituency is the best way to get both positive and negative input regarding our excellence. We will discuss issues of constituency at greater length in chapters 4, 10 and 12. Their satisfaction with our training efforts is the best validation of what is being done. Conversely, if our graduates and their communities are not happy with the results of our efforts, we certainly cannot affirm excellence in our training programs.

3. Governments or Governmentally Approved Agencies

There is affirmation of quality and excellence in official validation or accreditation processes. Increasingly governments reserve the right to "credential" or "charter" training programs. That doesn't restrict the right of churches or organizations to offer useful seminars and workshops. But governmental educational authorities want to make sure that those training efforts that call themselves "schools" are competent and structured to be schools. Government validation protects ordinary people against bogus training programs that offer cheap "degrees" with minimal work. These validation efforts do not normally meddle with the specifics of who serves as teacher, of who is taught or of what is taught in individual courses. Their concern is that those who teach are qualified, that the school has adequate facilities and funding, that the courses of study are designed for the degree being offered, that the program has a registered constitution and governing body, etc. For a variety of reasons, an evangelical training institution may opt not to be accredited or recognized by its government's educational ministries. However, most students place high value on attending a program that is "accredited," precisely because this implies an official acknowledgement of the program's quality and excellence.

4. Peer-level Training Institutions

Another way to verify excellence is through peer-level evaluation. This is especially useful for evangelical training institutions with goals that are very different from those of local universities. Governmental bodies are not in a position to assess how well we are doing in character formation or in effectively preparing people for ministry. However, this kind of evaluation can be done by colleagues who work in leadership training institutions at equivalent levels within the region. Such peer-level assessment is done formally through the accreditation agencies associated with International Council for Evangelical Theological Education (ICETE – www.icete-edu.org) and others. Those who have been involved in doing theological training are in the best position to propose standards for excellence in theological training as well as to help hold one another accountable for those standards. It is good when a program can be honored for its quality on a worldwide platform due to the recognition given by its peers.

5. The Staff and Leadership of the Training Institution Itself

All of those involved in evangelical theological leadership training need to sense whether or not they are doing a good job. In chapter 12 we will discuss how a training program can become a community that constantly renews and encourages itself to continue to grow in excellence. Every training program needs multiple ways to obtain feedback to learn from what it is doing. Being an excellent school requires excellence in many different areas. One good way for a program to assess its own excellence is to work through the self-evaluation review questions that are a part of formal accreditation visits.

Is Excellence Possible?

It's actually required! God's Word would not call us to excellence it if it were not possible. So to what extent are we aware of excellence because God is at work in us and through us? Do we have the eyes of God to understand the needs of people and their environment? Are our ministries well structured? Are we using our time wisely to do the right things in right ways? Are our dreams about things that are noble and profitable? Are we building our training on God's values, or are we unconsciously applying those cultural values that have shaped our past? Have we accommodated ourselves to mediocrity?

We assess our quality by knowing where we were supposed to be going and why, and then by reviewing the values and processes that helped us, by God's grace, to get to where we are now. How well have we responded to the needs of our context, given our goals and purposes? Did we accomplish what we intended? Are we satisfied with the processes we have been using to accomplish our goals? Can we say that what we actually did that which is good? How effectively have we used the resources that God has entrusted to us to do the task that he has given us to do? Knowing the answers to these kinds of questions helps us to affirm whether or not our leadership training institution is excellent, not only in the eyes of God, but before many others.

Conclusions

Training is a mandate that we have received from the Lord Jesus as part of his Great Commission to the whole church (Matt 28:18–20). The Apostle Paul encourages us with these words: "And whatever you do, whether in word or deed, do it all in the name of the Lord Jesus, giving thanks to God the Father through him" (Col 3:17). Those who give leadership to leadership training institutions need to discover what is or is not excellent in what they are doing. They need to know what to affirm as well as what to fix or even to drop as they work towards excellence.

As we will see throughout this book, excellent programs have good outcomes. They know where they are going and why. They meet minimum standards. They fit the context. Their purpose, process and product are all in accordance with biblical principles. They are governed, administered and staffed well. They are adequately resourced. Their communities are made up of competent and emotionally healthy people who know how to care for each other. Excellent theological institutions are learning communities that can renew themselves.

Discussion Questions Regarding Excellence

1. What do you understand by "excellence" in the training program of which you are a part?
2. In what ways have you sensed or seen God's "Well done, good and faithful servants" in what you are doing?
3. In what areas do you have a reputation for being good at what you do? How do you know this? Are there other areas where you actually have a public reputation for not being quite so good?

2

Excellence in Leadership

An excellent leadership training institution understands what leadership is and how it can be encouraged, trained and used. Good programs know how to take advantage of differing styles of leaders. Finding, encouraging and developing good leaders may be the most important piece of what makes a good program excellent.

Almost without exception, theological schools emerge from the vision and hard work of a charismatic leader. Schools wouldn't come into existence without their sacrificial work to develop administrative and curricular structures, to recruit teachers and students, and to find the resources to make the program work. However, this kind of singular charismatic leadership may not be a complete blessing to the school. Students and staff all seek the advice of their friend and leader, even when this means long delays in making decisions. It is difficult for anyone else to assume the leadership role from such charismatic people, especially given that founding leaders often continue on as trustees, as members of the governing board, as teachers and administrators and as the primary fund-raiser for the school. Although there often is great admiration and love for these very gifted people, such leaders tend to have a profound, even smothering, influence on everything.

What does your leadership look like? Many excellent books exist on the nature and practice of leadership. It is not my purpose to undertake a thorough review of good things that have already been said by others. In the bibliography at the end of this chapter I have listed some of the more significant books and articles on the subject. Yet what is amazing is how few leadership training schools have taken time to discuss what it is that *they* mean by "leadership." In what sense can a leadership training program train leaders if it isn't clear in its understanding of leadership?

In this chapter, we will examine what leadership is and isn't within the Scriptures, noting that who we are is always more important than what we do. We will not be considering the curricular questions of how to train our students for ministry as servant-leaders, since this will be discussed in chapter 6. Our concern in this chapter is with those who give leadership to leadership training programs. We need to consider the personality and quality traits that they need to have, as well as the specifics of what they need to do. How can these kinds of people be discovered or developed? What difference does it make that there are a variety of styles of leadership? Can such diversity in leadership work together in teams? We will examine these issues, noting that learning conflict-resolution skills is one important skill that any leader needs to have. We will also offer some suggestions as to how existing leadership can prepare for a transition to new leadership. One issue that we will not consider in this chapter is caring for and renewing the leaders that we have, as this will be covered in chapter 12.

What Is Leadership?

Is leadership a personal quality that someone is born with or a special gift that God bestows? Is it a positional role that puts a person up front, a job assigned for someone to do, or simply what occurs when a "leader" rises to the occasion in the midst of a crisis? Presumably all leaders don't follow the exact pattern of Moses, whose calling and extensive training were orchestrated by God himself over an eighty-year time span. Neither would it seem to be the norm for all leaders to spend a full forty years working in an internship program, as was the case with Joshua. But to what extent can leadership training be intentional – teaching skills and techniques that draw on a person's experiences and talents? Can leaders be trained by people who are not themselves leaders?

Our answers to these questions will have significant implications for our leadership training programs. If we perceive leadership as primarily a functional role into which most of our graduates will someday step, our training efforts should focus on providing practical skills, tools and resources to help the person lead well. The training should include words of wisdom from those who are leaders and who have been in leadership positions before and who understand something of the tasks that need to be done. Alternatively, if we conclude that "leadership" is primarily the use of gifts that God has given, our training efforts should help students come to a proper understanding of their gifts and abilities. It will also be fundamental to make sure that we are training the right people. The seeming paradox is that while we are aware that what a person acquires through educational experiences will not "produce" spiritual gifts, we do trust that our training efforts will help a person with leadership gifts to use those gifts more effectively.

Biblical Concepts of Leadership

The biblical words related to "lead" suggest that there is both a positional and a functional aspect to leadership. A leader is someone who is visibly up front and who takes people somewhere, whether leading God's people to the Promised Land or leading them astray! Moses was aware that God was the one who did the leading: "If the Lord is pleased with us, he will *lead* us into that land, a land flowing with milk and honey, and he will give it to us" (Num 14:8). Yet God gave part of the leadership task to Moses: "I am sending you to Pharaoh to *bring* my people the Israelites out of Egypt" (Exod 3:10). A leadership role was also given to Joshua: "Be strong and courageous, because you will *lead* these people to inherit the land I swore to their forefathers to give them" (Josh 1:6). In other words, God leads, the leader follows God and thus brings others to where God wants them to go.

Leading, or being in leadership, was a role filled by the prophets (e.g. Deborah in Judg 4:4), or by kings "like all the other nations . . . to *lead* us, to go out before us to fight our battles" (1 Sam 8:5). King Solomon prayed: "Give me wisdom and knowledge, that I may *lead* this people, for who is able to govern this great people of yours?" (2 Chr 1:10) Leadership was positional and involved a visible, up-front role, to help God's people accomplish something that God wanted done.

Leadership can be done badly – or it can be done well, but towards wrong ends. Both of these were problems for the people of Israel throughout their history. "O my people, your guides *lead* you astray, they turn you from the path" (Isa 3:12). This also was a problem in the church. The Apostle John warned: "I am writing these things to you about those who are trying to *lead* you astray" (1 John 2:26). Clearly, the blind should not be *led* by the blind (Matt 15:14). Jesus' purpose in coming into the world was "so that the blind will see" (John 9:39). Those who exercise leadership need to be able to see clearly. Leadership involves having vision, wisdom and understanding.

Christian leadership involves being a follower of Jesus. His words were not simply to be learned; they were to be obeyed (Matt 28:19). It is a good thing to ask God for guidance in knowing how to live. The disciples were taught to pray: "*Lead* us not into temptation, but deliver us from the evil one" (Matt 6:13). The Psalmist requested: "See if there is any offensive way in me, and *lead* me in the way everlasting" (Ps 139:24). As a result of what God was doing in him, the Psalmist could take responsibility for himself. "I will be careful to *lead* a blameless life" (Ps 101:2).

One important biblical image of leadership is that of a shepherd. God himself is a shepherd. David wrote: "He makes me lie down in green pastures; He *leads* me beside the quiet waters" (Ps 23:2). The promised Messiah was to be like this: "Then I will give you a shepherd after my own heart, who will *lead* you with knowledge and understanding" (Jer 3:15). The imagery applies to the risen Christ at the end of time: "For the Lamb at the center of the throne will be their shepherd. He will *lead* them to springs of living waters" (Rev 7:17). John describes Jesus as the great "I Am" who is both the door for the flock and its shepherd: "The watchman opens the gate for him, and the sheep listen to his voice. He calls his own sheep by name and *leads* them out" (John 10:3).

An exhaustive study of the biblical words used for leaders has been done by David Bennett.[1] In a summary of *Metaphors of Ministry* given at the Consultation on Institutional Development for Theological Education in the Two-Thirds World (26 June–8 July 1995), he made the following observations about some of what leadership is not:

- Jesus never used any of the many words made up of the root arch – words related to ruling and authority.
- Although Jesus told many stories about masters and servants, he never compared his followers to the masters – only to the servants.

---

1. David Bennett, *Metaphors of Ministry: Biblical Images for Leaders and Followers* (Grand Rapids, MI: Baker Book House, 1993).

- Jesus described his followers as a family, but never suggested that any of them take on the role of "father."
- When Jesus referred to his disciples as pastors or shepherds, the emphasis was on caring for the flock, not on the authority the shepherd had. Jesus did not train his disciples to be future chiefs who would be giving orders to the whole universe.
- A group of images that are notable by their absence are those that come from the temple and worship. The disciples were to be brothers, and it is possible that Jesus wanted to avoid any suggestion of "eliteness" among them.

Jesus' disciples were not to become like the rulers of the Gentiles, "lording it over" others in their "exercise of authority" over them (Mark 10:42). According to Jesus, "Whoever wants to become great among you must be your servant, and whoever wants to be first must be slave to all" (Mark 8:43–44). The Apostle Peter understood these words and reflected them back in advice given to elders much later in his own life: "Be shepherds of God's flock that is under your care, serving as overseers – not because you must, but because you are willing, as God wants you to be; not greedy for money, but eager to serve; not lording it over those entrusted to you, but being examples to the flock" (1 Pet 5:2–3). Being a servant to the flock does not mean that there are no specific leadership roles, as some were given the task of being elders, overseers and shepherds. But there clearly are wrong ways to exercise leadership. No one should be forced into a leadership role, nor should it be taken on as a way to gain power or money. Leadership involves being a servant, caring pastorally for those being led.

In Romans 12, leadership is called a gift, one that relates to the administration of people. If one's gift is "leadership, let him govern diligently" (Rom 12:8). This is only one gift among many as all of God's people are gifted for some sort of ministry. There are undoubtedly aspects of leadership with the use of any of the gifts that God has given. God arranged the parts of the body "just as he wanted them to be" (1 Cor 12:18). People may not exclude themselves from ministry because they don't see themselves as leaders due to their perception of not having the right gifts. Neither can people (including those who are gifted as leaders) consider themselves to be so multi-talented that they have no need of others. According to Paul in Ephesians 4, the whole body, joined and held together by every supporting ligament, only "grows and builds itself up in love" when "each part does its work" (Eph 4:16). Leadership involves using one's gifts in administering people for the good of the whole body of Christ.

It is in this context that we read of something special that God did for his church. He "gave" some people to the church, each of whom had his or her own special gifting: apostles, prophets, evangelists and pastor-teachers. These were people recognized as leaders. Yet their task was not to do the work of the kingdom on behalf of others, but to prepare or equip God's people so that they could do the work of the ministry (Eph 4:11–12). Leadership involves helping equip other people to get ministry done.

From a biblical perspective, effective leadership involves qualities of life, and is not simply a position or role to fill. We may conclude that leadership involves:

- being a follower of Jesus.
- taking people somewhere.
- having vision, wisdom and understanding.
- being a servant, caring pastorally for those that are being led.
- using one's gifts for the good of the whole body of Christ.
- helping equip others to get ministry done.

Character: Who a Leader Needs to Be

Who we are is more important than what we do. Performance alone is not what matters, whether in leadership or in any other sort of ministry. In Jesus' Sermon on the Mount, the false teacher is not rejected on the basis of his teaching per se, but by the fruits of his life (Matt 7:15–20). Neither was Jesus impressed by those who called him "Lord" or by those who did incredible things in his name, such as prophesying, doing great miracles or casting out demons. What mattered was obedience, doing "the will of the Father" (Matt 7:21). Jesus told a story of two men who built identical houses, one on a rock and the other on sand. Both could have been Bible school students, as they both heard the words of Jesus adequately enough to have passed Bible exams with excellent marks. Both apparently had equivalent skills and experience in construction, and both were working from the same blueprint. What made them wise or foolish was not their knowledge, gifts, skills or their faithfulness to the blueprint. The "foundational" point was their obedience, "putting the words of Jesus into practice" (Matt 7:24).

Oswald Sanders, in *Spiritual Leadership*,[2] presents the following list as essential qualities needed in any leader, including those who give administrative guidance and leadership to theological training programs.

- Discipline – learning to obey
- Vision – seeing possibilities and understanding their implications with optimism
- Wisdom – discerning the right application of knowledge in moral and spiritual areas
- Decision – decisively making decisions once all the facts are in hand
- Courage – facing difficulties without fear or depression
- Humility – realistically understanding who he or she is in Christ
- Humor – without being at the expense of others
- Anger – at injustices that dishonor God and that leave people in slavery
- Patience – maintaining solid relationships, not going in front of everyone else
- Friendship – loving people, encouraging the best in them
- Tact and Diplomacy – juggling various viewpoints while respecting the person
- Motivation – inspiring others to service
- Executive Ability – stewardship so that everything is done decently

Many of these factors are character traits that should be found in any follower of Jesus. We cannot overemphasize the importance of character in leadership. Who we are communicates what we feel is important more than anything that we might say. If our most important values are neatness or order, without saying much, our students may learn more about not walking on the grass than they ever will about loving relationships or being ready for the return of Jesus. Our professional competence as teachers or administrators goes hand in hand with our attitudes and relationships. Students learn from observing who we are and how we do ministry more than they do from our handouts. What Jesus said is true, both positively and negatively, "A student

---

2. Oswald Sanders, *Spiritual Leadership* (Chicago, IL: Moody Press, 1967), chapters 7–8.

is not above his teacher, but everyone who is fully trained will be *like* his teacher" (Luke 6:40).

One's life lived in the context of community is the most important aspect of leadership (or any other ministry). Who we are as leaders, teachers and staff is what matters the most in a theological education program. Our educational task is not primarily functional, that is, teaching skills or techniques that a student can use in "doing" his or her ministry. Neither is our task primarily to help students acquire quantities of background knowledge and information about theology, history or the Scriptures. The primary task of theological education is to shape the lives of those who are followers of Jesus so that they can be used by God as leaders and influencers for the good of his kingdom. Character matters, which is why leaders of leadership training programs primarily "teach" by who they are.

Responsibilities: What a Leader Needs to Do

I once asked a group of about fifty theological education leaders at a workshop to list qualities or characteristics that they felt should exist in those who lead theological education programs. Their responses indicated that character was indeed important. A leader should be a person with integrity, vision, passion, a love for God and people, an accessible listener, yet one able to make decisions. Background experience also mattered, with the assumption that a leader has the requisite skills to actually do the job. It mattered that a leader understands his or her cultural context. As to job skills, what seemed most significant was that a leader could work with people. That meant hiring the right people and releasing the wrong ones, as well as knowing how to build healthy relationships both internally and externally. A good leader should be an encourager, equipper, problem-solver and delegator.

There are four basic tasks for those who give leadership to leadership training programs:

1. A Leader Provides Vision and a Plan

As we noted earlier, leadership involves getting people somewhere. So, those who give leadership to leadership training programs need vision and focus to know where they are going. Leaders know that leadership training is strategic for the growth and maturity of the church. They are convinced that training programs are exciting places where lives are being shaped for God's glory and where future leaders are being effectively equipped to make a difference for the kingdom of God. Leaders need goals and a plan to know how to get from here to there. These are issues that we will discuss further in chapter 3.

2. A Leader Builds, Equips and Encourages Teams

Leaders must find those who share their vision. People with competence, enthusiasm and credibility need to be recruited for training programs to have functional boards, an administrative and financial team that will discover and properly use adequate funding for the program, and a teaching team with competency and with lives that will illustrate what is being taught. Leaders should not simply do things for others (which could be manipulative) or on behalf of others (which could be paternalistic, and probably not very productive), but through others. To function as a team, relationships matter. All people need to be empowered, equipped and encouraged.

3. A Leader Teaches and Master Teaches

Those who give leadership to leadership training programs must have the pedagogical skills to help adults to learn and grow. They will want to do some teaching to keep in touch with their skills and with the real world of their students. However, what may be even more important for a leader is to become a master teacher, helping others to gain skills in effective teaching.

4. A Leader Represents the School Publicly

In the eyes of the community, government, churches, faculty, staff and students, leaders embody the school. The kind of character and skills expected in graduates is what is expected to be visible in the program's leaders. Leaders will find ways to be accessible and to minister publicly so as to be able to listen to feedback and to share stories of what God is doing. They will assume their roles in building a solid funding base and in representing the program wherever they can.

Discovering and Developing Leadership

How do we discover those who are gifted at taking people somewhere and who have the gifts and skills to assume leadership roles? Perhaps the simplest answer is through observing the lives of others. As Jesus said, "It is by their fruits that we know them" (Matt 7:16). We need to look around to see who it is that cares about where others are going. Who have good relational skills? Who have lives worth imitating? Who have vision and skills in teaching or administrating others? Who have a track record of helping others to get or keep moving, without manipulating them? We need to notice those that God is already using as leaders, and then find ways to encourage them as they grow.

This doesn't require mastering *Leadership for Dummies* (if there is such a book), or applying the *10 Proven Steps Towards Becoming a Perfect Leader*. Learning to learn is one of the most important skills that anyone can possess, including a leader. Becoming a leader is a process and takes effort and time. The best way to help potential leaders to grow in character and ministry skills is through finding experienced leaders with skills and a willingness to serve as mentors. Leaders-in-process will benefit from a number of different relationships with people who will teach or disciple them, who will coach or counsel them, who will sponsor them to others and who will be models for them.

Laurent Daloz describes three important things that mentors do:

1. **Mentors provide support.** Through listening, being an advocate and by sharing of one's own experience, the mentor provides a comfortable structure in which people can learn to learn from their own present experiences.
2. **Mentors challenge.** A skillful teacher or mentor helps others to rethink fundamental assumptions and understand situations or problems in different ways. A mentor helps people set high, though realistic, expectations for themselves.
3. **Mentors Provide Vision.** By providing feedback and encouragement, a mentor encourages critical reflection and self-awareness to help people see what they can (and should) become.[3]

---

3. Laurent Daloz, *Mentor: Guiding the Journey of Adult Learners* (San Francisco, CA: Jossey-Bass, 1999), 206–229.

For most of us, our best teachers were those who wanted us to figure things out for ourselves. Accordingly, a good mentor is a guide who works with a potential leader to put together an individual learning plan. Mentors find ways for potential leaders to immerse themselves in leadership tasks and then ask questions that require reflection on new experiences and knowledge. Mentors are most effective when they can be available regularly to listen to things that are being learned as well as to respond to the questions that people have. Good leaders who serve as mentors will help potential leaders to continue to adapt and grow within their own unique learning styles.

Styles and Varieties of Leadership

Leadership style is how leaders help people get the job done. There is no single profile of what a leader ought to be. Neither is there only one way in which leadership happens. Leadership can focus on a task (getting something done), on process (doing things in the right ways) or on people (enriching or encouraging those who work under or for the leader). All of these things are important, just different.

Each of us is a unique combination of abilities, interests and backgrounds – working with people who are equally unique in their gifts, responsibilities and competence. We come from different cultures and work in a variety of contexts. We may hold similar values, but prioritize them differently. Some leaders are great at the big picture, dreaming huge visions. Others function better as cheerleaders, coaches, facilitators, problem solvers or executive managers. Note just some of the varieties of leadership found in the Scriptures.

- Moses – An intermediary who led through a spokesperson.
- Nehemiah – One who made the project work, even forcing right behavior on occasion.
- David – The king, at the top with all authority.
- Peter – An impetuous doer who took people with him.
- Paul – A team player, or delegator. "I plant, someone else waters."

It is good for those who are in leadership roles to discover their own unique styles of leadership. We need to know how to lead from what we are good at, as well as to know where we are not so strong. None of us were created or gifted to be omnicompetent, and it is healthy to know where we really do need the help of others to get the right things done.

Several good tools have been developed for the business world to help people identify their leadership styles. One common tool is the Myers-Brigg indicator grid[4] which is based on how people learn, make decisions or relate to those around them.[5] Another commonly used tool called the DISC model (www.intesiresources.com) describes behavioral patterns in terms of strengths and weaknesses in four areas: Dominance (those who are risk-takers, forceful, and direct), Influence (those who are emotional and gregarious and who attempt to influence others through talking and activity), Steadiness or Security (those who are predictable, loyal team players, who like a steady pace) and Conscientiousness or Conformity (those who like adhering to rules and structures and who want to do things right the first time).

Leadership implies followers. We sometimes assume that leadership must be what is done by big people "at the top." The reality is that most people take on leadership roles at some point in their lives. Leadership is done by pioneers (who go ahead of everyone else), by prophets (who call people back to something important), or by managers (who help people get the job done efficiently). Shepherds go in front of the sheep. Sheep dogs do their work from the back and along the sides. A lot of sheep seem to love team leadership as a way of doing things together. Hopefully in all these cases, the flock moves in the right direction.

Our conclusion is that there are many different acceptable styles of leadership and that leadership is done best when we work together and when we are all moving in the right direction.

Working Together as a Team

Most leaders are absolutely overwhelmed by all that falls on their shoulders. A person may be competent enough in what he or she is doing – but there is just too much to be done! Most of us need to listen carefully (again) to the admonition that Jethro gave Moses: "What you are doing is not good. You and these people who come to you will only wear yourselves out. The work is too heavy for you, you cannot handle it alone" (Exod 18:17–18).

---

4. http://en.wikipedia.org/wiki/Meyers_Briggs

5. Renee Baron, *What Type Am I? The Myers-Brigg Indicator Made Easy* (New York, NY: Penguin, 1998).

We are supposed to do things together. God gave Adam a partner in the Garden of Eden because it was "not good for the man to be alone" (Gen 2:18). We are a collection of living stones being built by God into a spiritual house (1 Pet 2:5). We are fellow citizens and members of God's household, God's holy temple (Eph 2:19-22). We "are the body of Christ and each one of [us] is a part of it" (1 Cor 12:27). We only grow when each part of that body does what it is supposed to do (Eph 4:16). Even God himself exists in community: Father, Son and Holy Spirit.

Leaders are not supposed to "do" the work of ministry, but to help equip others to do that work. How can those giving leadership to theological education programs put these principles in practice for their own good, as well as for the good of their institutions?

More committees or random "work groups" is not the solution. Delegation can help. But what is key in good delegation is determining what can and should be done by others. This involves rethinking our job descriptions. We then empower others and trust them to do what really is theirs to do. Leadership doesn't need to be done by committee. But shared responsibilities by a leadership team committed to a common goal can be a great idea.

In *Team Players and Teamwork* (San Francisco: Jossey-Bass, 1990) Glen Parker suggests that it can be helpful to have people on a leadership team who bring different perspectives and styles to a group. Parker suggests (p. 164) that there are four basic types of team players:

- **Contributors** – people who are organized, logical, pragmatic and systematic, though they also can be perfectionists, data-bound, uncreative and short-sighted.
- **Collaborators** – those who are visionary, imaginative, open, flexible and conceptual, though they can be too global, over-ambitious, insensitive and unaware of reality.
- **Communicators** – those who are supportive, relational, tactful, patient and relaxed, though they may be impractical, aimless, manipulative and even foolish.
- **Challengers** – those who are principled, ethical and candid. They question everything, though they can also be nitpickers, rigid, even self-righteous and arrogant.

Leadership teams function best when they have at least one of each type. We will discover the joys of synergy as we discover how to work with one another in community using the multiple gifts that God has given us. We also will survive longer with less emotional and physical burnout.

Resolving Tensions and Conflict

Conflict is inevitable in any organization. It can occur when people want the same position, ministry and privileges or when there are differing views concerning solutions or priorities. Frustrations can arise because of unfulfilled expectations or when leadership doesn't work well. Sometimes attitudes and personalities clash. People react when they feel underappreciated or that they have been treated unfairly.

Donald C. Palmer points out that there are often substantive issues involved in conflict, such as:
- Conflicts over values, beliefs and traditions
- Conflicts over purposes and goals
- Conflicts over programs and methods
    - How should we do it? Strategy, methods, program
    - Who should do it? Organization, team
    - When should we do it? Schedule
    - How much should it cost? Budget
- Conflicts over the facts, objectivity and perspective
- Conflicts over ministry vision, personalities and leadership style.[6]

Not all conflict is sinful. It can be a healthy indication of life and vitality in an organization as creative people suggest new ideas and changes that need to be made. Conflict is only dangerous when it is not resolved, allowing for resentments to build up. Leadership is crucial in helping to make sure that there are processes in place so that people are listened to and issues are appropriately dealt with.

Our students will learn how to resolve conflicts as they watch their leaders deal with conflict. There are at least two unhealthy ways to respond to conflict: (1) try to escape from it or deny that it even exists; or (2) attack one's enemies – verbally, legally or physically.[7]

---

6. Donald C. Palmer, *Managing Conflict Creatively: A Guide for Missionaries and Christian Workers* (Pasadena, CA: William Carey Library, 1990), 11–13.

7. Peacemaker Ministries, P.O. Box 81130, Billings, MT 59108 USA. www.HisPeace.org

Peacemakers Ministries suggest four steps that will help to resolve conflict.

1. Instead of focusing on us and our hurts, we should rejoice in the Lord and in his forgiveness as we seek to faithfully obey his commands.
2. Instead of blaming others for a conflict, we should take responsibility for our own contribution to conflicts.
3. Instead of pretending that conflict does not exist, or talking behind people's backs, we should either overlook minor offenses or talk personally with those who have offended us.
4. Instead of allowing premature compromise or allowing relationships to wither, we should actively pursue genuine peace and reconciliation.

Leaders of leadership training programs should learn how to use conflict for good and for change. May they know how to encourage healthy communities where forgiveness is practiced. "Blessed are the peacemakers, for they will be called the children of God" (Matt 5:9).

Negotiating Leadership Transition

One of the hardest things for many leaders is preparing for the next generation of leaders. This can be as difficult in schools or the church as it is in some governments. Rarely do people have enough common sense to realize when it is right for them to step down voluntarily and allow others to give leadership to the organization. It is important to plan for transition, and not let this become a crisis after the leader finally dies.

All leaders should be actively mentoring and encouraging new leaders. Nevertheless, I am not convinced that it is a good idea for leaders of theological training programs to be the ones who select their own successors. This is better left to the school's governing body, which can prayerfully and carefully examine the qualifications of a number of people in the light of the purpose, needs and opportunities facing the training program.

It can be helpful to have periods of overlap between the old and the new leadership so that the new provost, principal or president may observe the many details of the program before having to assume complete responsibility for it. However, in general, a transition should be as short and clean as possible. Even though it is good to thoroughly understanding one's task before having to take it on, not everyone wants (like Joshua) to serve as an assistant for forty years before assuming leadership responsibilities.

Two issues are important in a leadership transition. The first is that new leadership know how to appropriately honor the work of the one who was in leadership before. Even if there is a collective sigh of relief when the old leader finally steps down (or dies), there is nothing gained by saying negative things about the past. However, it is imperative that new leadership have the freedom and authority to do new things, and not simply be forced to carry on traditions that may no longer be appropriate to the needs and realities of the program now. Although wisdom suggests that not everything needs to be completely changed the day after a leadership transition, there must be freedom to move appropriately into a new era in the life of the school. That usually requires that the retiring leader not stay around to watch or to give advice.

Conclusions

Theological education programs come in many different sizes, shapes and forms. Giving leadership to leadership training programs is not an easy job. Yet without excellence in those who serve as leaders to our training institutions, there will not be much excellence in the rest of the program. It is our privilege to help equip those that God has gifted and called into ministry. We can't distribute spiritual gifts on God's behalf, but we can help an administrator to administrate more effectively; a teacher to teach better; and a pastor to develop a whole package of pastoral skills. May your training institution have excellent leadership to allow you to do this!

Discussion Questions Regarding Your Leadership

1. How well are you preparing for the future leadership needs of your school? How do you (or could you) discover people with leadership potential? Do you have a process for selecting and preparing those who will assume leadership roles in your training program? If so, how well does it work?

2. What key values do you hold concerning leadership? What models illustrate these values? What stories can you tell about people who illustrate these values?
3. What are the leadership roles most predominant in your culture? What leadership styles do you currently have on your leadership team? To what extent are different styles of leadership valid or appropriate to your context?
4. What do your leaders actually do? Review the various job descriptions that you have. Given the importance of issues of character, how could you strengthen one another in who you are?
5. How well does your leadership team work as a team? What could help you to function better?
6. What is the role of leadership in the resolution of problems and in the renewing of relationships? What pieces of conflict resolution are beyond the control of a leader?

Suggestions for Further Reading

Anderson, Terry D. *Transforming Leadership: Equipping Yourself and Coaching Others to Build the Leadership Organization.* New York, NY: St. Lucie Press, 1998.

Augsburger, David W. *Conflict Mediation across Cultures: Pathways and Patterns.* Louisville, KY: Westminster/John Knox Press, 1992.

Banks, Robert, and Kimberly Powell, eds. *Faith in Leadership.* San Francisco, CA: Jossey-Bass, 2000.

Bennett, David W. *Metaphors of Ministry: Biblical Images for Leaders and Followers.* Grand Rapids, MI: Baker Book House, 1993.

Bennis, Warren. *The Unconscious Conspiracy: Why Leaders Can't Learn to Lead.* AMA-COM, 1976.

Blanchard, Kenneth, and Spencer Johnson. *The One-Minute Manager.* New York, NY: Berkley Books, 1982.

Covey, Stephen R. *The 8th Habit.* New York, NY: Simon and Schuster, 2005.

———. *The Seven Habits of Highly Effective People.* New York, NY: Simon and Schuster, 1989.

Clinton, J. Robert. *The Making of a Leader: Recognizing the Lessons and Stages of Leadership Development.* Colorado Springs, CO: Nav Press, 1988.

Collins, Jim. *Good to Great.* New York, NY: Harper Collins Publishers, 2001.

Daloz, Laurent. *Mentor: Guiding the Journey of Adult Learners*. San Francisco, CA: Jossey-Bass, 1999.

DePree, Max. *Leadership is an Art*. New York, NY: Bantam, Doubleday Dell Publishing, 1989.

Drucker, Peter F. *The Effective Executive*. New York, NY: Harper and Row, 1985.

Early, Gene. "The Chief Executive Role as God's Classroom for Character Formation." *Transformation* 18, no. 1 (2001): 9ff.

———. "A Second Generation Leader Succeeds the Founder: What is the Process?" *Transformation* 18, no. 1 (2001): 1ff.

Elmer, Duane. *Cross-Cultural Conflict: Building Relationships for Effective Ministry*. Downers Grove, IL: InterVarsity, 1993.

Ford, Leighton. *Transforming Leadership: Jesus' Way of Creating Vision, Shaping Values, and Empowering Change*. Downers Grove, IL: InterVarsity, 1991.

Fullan, Michael. *Leading in a Culture of Change*. San Francisco, CA: Jossey-Bass, 2001.

Gardner, John W. *On Leadership*. New York, NY: Free Press, 1990.

Greenleaf, Robert K. *Servant Leadership*. New York, NY: Paulist Press, 1977.

Hesselbein, Francis, and Paul M. Cohen, eds. *Leader to Leader: Enduring Insights on Leadership from the Drucker Foundation's Award-Winning Journal*. San Francisco, CA: Jossey-Bass, 1999.

Hesselbein, Francis, Marshall Goldsmith, and Tichard Beckhard. *The Leader of the Future*. San Francisco, CA: Jossey-Bass, 1996.

Jennings, Ken, and John Stahl-Wert. *The Serving Leader*. San Francisco, CA: Berrett-Koehler Publishers, Inc, 2003.

Kouzes, James W., and Barry Z. Posner. *The Leadership Challenge*. San Francisco, CA: Jossey-Bass, 1995.

Lewis, Phillip V. *Transformational Leadership: A New Model for Total Church Involvement*. Nashville, TN: Broadman & Holman Publishers, 1996.

Marshall, Tom. *Understanding Leadership*. Grand Rapids, MI: Baker, 2003.

Maxwell, John C. *The 21 Irrefutable Laws of Leadership*. Nashville, TN: Thomas Nelson, 1998.

———. *The Winning Attitude: Your Pathway to Personal Success*. Nashville, TN: Thomas Nelson, 1993.

Osei-Mensah, Gottfried. "Leaders: What Are They?" *SPAN – IFES in English and Portuguese Speaking Africa* 2, no. 1 (January–April 1997).

Palmer, Donald C. *Managing Conflict Creatively: A Guide for Missionaries and Christian Workers*. Pasadena, CA: William Carey Library, 1990.

Parker, Glenn M. *Team Players and Teamwork: The New Competitive Business Strategy.* San Francisco, CA: Jossey-Bass, 1990.

Peters, Thomas J., and Robert H Waterman, Jr. *In Search of Excellence: Lessons from America's Best-Run Companies.* New York, NY: Warner Books, 1982.

Ratzburg, Wilf. "The Blanchard Leadership Model," from *Organizational Behavior* – OBNotes.htm (http://www.geocities.com/ Athens/Forum/1650/html blanchard.html).

Sanders, J. Oswald. *Spiritual Leadership.* Chicago, IL: Moody Press, 1967.

Snook, Stewart G. *Developing Leaders through TEE: Case Studies from Africa.* Wheaton, IL: Billy Graham Center, 1992.

Stanley, Paul D., and J. Robert Clinton. *Connecting: The Mentoring Relationship You Need to Succeed in Life.* Colorado Springs, CO: NavPress, 1992.

Wivcharuck, Peter. *Building Effective Leadership: A Guide to Christian and Professional Management.* Alberta, Canada: International Christian Leadership Development Foundation, 1987.

3

Excellence in Strategic Planning

Without a clear idea of where one is going, it is difficult to know whether or not anything is being accomplished. An excellent leadership training institution takes the time to develop and routinely review a strategic plan that includes discovering its values, defining its mission in the light of needs, assessing its own strengths and weaknesses and then prayerfully dreaming in order to develop a doable plan that takes it to where it ought to go.

I was once asked by a church, "If we were to give you US $10,000, what would you do with it?" I don't really think that they were intending to give me a check, but they did want to know if I had a strategy for ministry, and whether I had any clue as to what my plan might cost.

Having a workable plan is important for theological education programs. Bible schools and seminaries are attempting to equip men and women with the knowledge and skills needed for effective ministry. The process involves acquiring biblical knowledge and the theological insights of the ages. It includes gaining an understanding of how truth can be applied practically in a real world. It involves conscious character and spiritual development so that our graduates illustrate what truth is.

Accomplishing this is an immense task. Each student is uniquely gifted and is moving towards a unique ministry within a unique context. We don't have all the resources in the world. We are often inadequately staffed, and what staff and faculty we have is composed of imperfect people. To complicate things even further, we typically only have three to four years with which to work in any given student's life. So, how can we possibly use our resources, tools and people to accomplish something significant for the kingdom of God? How should we prioritize the choices that we have to make? For all this, we need a well-thought-through and comprehensive strategic plan. Excellent training programs have strategic plans which serve as guides for all that they do.

In this chapter we will consider what strategic planning is and is not. We will then look at five steps which are needed, prior to writing a strategic plan and in the regular review of an existing plan. These are: (1) identify your core values, (2) revisit your mission statement, (3) do a needs assessment, (4) conduct an institutional assessment of your strengths, weaknesses and resources, and (5) dream and pray about what can and should be strengthened, dropped or added.

What Strategic Planning Is Not

1. Strategic Planning Is Not Trying to Do Everything That Someone Somewhere Might Need

Any given Bible school cannot be all things to all people. So, exactly what is it that you are noted for and are really good at? How has God used you in the past? Who are you serving? A good strategic plan defines questions of constituency and reflects how that specific constituency will be well served by who you are and what you do.

2. Strategic Planning Is Not Simply Perfecting What Was Inherited from Your Past

For a fair number of programs in the non-Western world, their primary purpose seems to be to ensure that that which always has been, forevermore shall be, amen. Even though they may be aware (sometimes even painfully aware) that the program was developed during colonial days by foreigners drawing on their Western models of education, what exists now is sacred, requiring only that it be preserved and polished. Any change in what has always been is perceived to be a betrayal of the loving labor of the founders. Consequently, the driving energy of strategic planning for the institution comes in perpetuating and perfecting what was originally intended to be. The sad piece of this is that there is a good chance that if the founders could set the program up today, they would use creative newer models of learning, just like they did when they started the program. Strategic planning cannot simply be polishing relics. Although there are indeed many good things to affirm from our past, strategic planning needs to consider the realities of the present. As our students change and the world in which they minister changes, so also do our training institutions and their programs need to change. Strategic planning balances an affirmation of the past with the challenges of the present.

3. Strategic Planning Is Not Merely Fixing What Is Broken

Just as in an old house, people, programs and facilities in Bible schools can wear out and fall apart. It is not a bad idea to keep a running list of everything that is not going well, and then to come up with a "plan" to fix it. However, if doing this kind of ongoing maintenance is all that we do when we "plan," we may be missing some of the bigger issues. Certain course offerings or study programs shouldn't be fixed; they should be dropped. Some buildings shouldn't be patched; they should be replaced. Some teachers and administrators . . .

Although we need to give attention to making things work well, a strategic plan encompasses much more than just fixing things. We must look at the broader impact of all that we are and all that we have. A good strategic plan includes maintenance issues, but only as a part of our overall program.

4. Strategic Planning Is Not Creating New Academic Programs

Some schools seem to think that a "strategic plan" means launching a variety of new "upper-level programs." The rationale is that these reflect student and community desires within the educational development of the region in general. Accordingly, much time, energy and funding is spent creatively adapting and establishing MA, ThM or PhD programs. Each new program may be valid, but in and of itself, developing a new degree program is not what we mean by strategic planning. A strategic plan looks at current program strengths and successes in the light of the real needs of our students and the world in which they are and will be ministering. As we think through what can be done with the limited resources that we have (people, facilities, library, funding), realistically, how many programs can we afford to offer? If we introduce new programs, to what extent might this mean that the quality programs that have given our school such a good reputation in the past might no longer function as well as they have? Do churches and Christian organizations need the graduates of the newer or the older programs – or both? A good strategic plan builds on a school's proven strengths as it responds to the real needs of its environment within the resources that it has.

5. Strategic Planning Is Not Preparing Blueprints for Buildings

For too many leadership training programs, it seems that being healthy is calculated only in terms of numerical growth. Thus the strategic plan becomes a public relations document with colorful graphs showing projections of growth over the next five to ten years in programs, students, books, faculty and buildings. Most of the pages of this plan are used to present sketches and cost estimates for all the new buildings (and perhaps even the new campus) that will be needed to accommodate the projected growth. Admittedly, campus development is a valid part of a strategic plan. Nevertheless, being strategic does not necessarily mean being bigger. Even if growth does seem to be important to the institution's development, a strategic plan needs to be carefully based on research and reality, not simply on imagined or hoped-for increases. Furthermore, a strategic plan must consider the many other factors that inevitably accompany growth in student numbers or in the number of degree-level programs, such as library development, qualified national faculty, staff support, student recruitment, administrative costs and so forth. A good strategic plan is not only comprehensive; it is based on reality.

6. Strategic Planning Is Not a Document Written by a Very Small Committee

To work well, strategic planning needs to be a group process. Preparing a five-year or a ten-year plan is not like a research paper to be submitted to the administration or the board. Neither is it the private plan of the principal, the administrative team or the board. A plan that is strategic needs to reflect the collective dreams of everyone. It revises and renews things that everyone perceives as needing revision and renewal. It suggests the creation of new programs for which there is a broad felt need. So, while it is a good idea to appoint a working committee to coordinate the strategic planning process, and even to have a highly perceptive person with communications skills in charge of compiling the results, a good strategic plan is owned and developed by just about everyone in the institution as well as by the institution's stakeholders.

Developing a Strategic Plan
1. Identify Your Core Values

It may seem odd to start with the question of values. The reality is that everything we do ultimately reflects what is important to us. Whether consciously or not, our plans and actions demonstrate what values we have. Accordingly, before developing specific plans for the future of a leadership training program, it is worth the time to revisit and reaffirm what it is that is important to everyone involved – your staff, faculty, the governing board, even your students.

Note that values are not necessarily Bible verses about spiritual traits or fruits. These things should indeed be important to you, but values also include expectations of the way people dress, how we relate to each other, and how we picture what learning should look like. In almost all of this, values reflect what is important to our cultures. That may or may not be a good thing.

Some values are more important to us than others, as any marriage illustrates. What was important within the family of one of the partners may not have been important at all in the family of the other. When disagreements arise, it is worth reflecting on why the thing matters so much to us. The deepest conflicts normally emerge when values clash. Frankly, some things are worth fighting for. In most Bible schools, denominations, organizations and families, important battles have been fought. We need to discern what it is that was (and is) so important that it was worth fighting for.

In a similar way, identifying our heroes (and enemies) can be a useful exercise for discovering our values. What is it about these people that made them so important to us, either positively or negatively? Why does their opinion matter so much to us?

The potential for value clashes is greater when we come from different places. For North Americans, efficiency is terribly important, as "time is money!" However, for Latin Americans, relationships are generally much more important than time. In trying to obey God, a Brazilian student might choose to stay up all night with a hurting relative or friend rather than finish a term paper due the next day. To what extent is this right or wrong? In our planning, how can we give appropriate space to the differing values held by our students and teachers?

In an African world, the good of the community is an important value. It also matters that one respects the authority of a person who is an elder, even if he or she does not have much formal training. Scripture affirms that giving respect and maintaining unity are biblical values. However, for Americans and many Europeans, being right and defending one's rights (and the rights of others) is what matters, irrespective of the age, gender, race or religion of the person involved. Western Christian culture suggests that since each person is made in the image of God, everyone should develop his or her gifts to the fullest, irrespective of what the community thinks about this.

These are the kinds of values that will clash, even educationally. Should exams and the grading process focus on individual achievements or should there be assignments that help students to work together in teams? To what extent should a teacher or administrator have to explain himself or herself to anyone – ever? Should the staff take tea with the students, or should there be separate tea rooms and tea times? Do our values (and the culture) require that there be more space (and opulence) for the offices of full professors than for associate professors, who have more space than junior lecturers, who have more space than assistant lecturers, who have more space than teaching aides, and so forth? Or will a well-oiled hierarchical system communicate all too clearly to our students the importance of having status and requiring respect and comfort once *they* become clergy? For that matter, how does status dictate what student housing should look like now?

What we believe and hold dear will inevitably influence what our students really learn, whether it was intended to be taught or not. Our views on community, cleanliness, being on time, purity, piety, reconciliation, forgiveness, the role of the Holy Spirit in learning, etc. – how we feel about all of these will necessarily affect what really gets learned by our students. We need to discover what our values are so that the planning that we do for our programs and educational communities will consciously and carefully build on what is important to us. Part of this process should inevitably involve evaluating (and even discarding) those inherited cultural values that we already hold, some of which may not be biblical. In order to be intentional in what you accomplish by your training efforts, begin your strategic planning process by identifying and evaluating your core values.

2. Revisit Your Mission Statement

Much has been written about developing mission or purpose statements. Essentially this is a summary of what you are as a training program. A mission statement should succinctly answer the following questions:
- Who are you?
- Why do you exist?
- For whom (or for what) do you exist?
- How do you intend to do what you will do?
- Where will you do it? And for how long?

Almost every school already has some sort of purpose or mission statement. Before jumping to revise, fix or create this, it may be useful to organize a variety of small groups who will systematically work their way through the big and little aspects of your entire program in the light of what your mission statement currently says. Is it all there? Does the statement reflect what you are trying to do and be? Does it reflect all of your values and what is important to you?

Taking your mission statement seriously means asking questions like: "Are there activities currently being done that go beyond our mission statement?" If so, part of your strategic plan should include eliminating such activities since they do not contribute to what you really intend to do. Alternatively, if you conclude that the extraneous activities are simply too "important" to be dropped, you need to rewrite your mission statement.

Does your mission statement suggest new activities or entire areas of ministry that you have never done? If so, then the strategic plan needs to sketch out how to begin something that is important to what you are as a training institution. A good mission statement will be inclusive, covering everything you do or will do. It will also be limiting, defining what you don't or won't do.

One of the more important aspects of both developing and refining a mission statement is the involvement of the broader community. Admittedly, someone brilliant could draft the ideal mission statement for your training program. However, one person's construct (especially if that person is someone with authority) should not be allowed to become so sacred that it cannot be challenged, discussed or changed.

A good mission statement will be a concise (even memorizable) summary of what your program is all about. As a summary, it is a point of reference against which your program can be evaluated. Do all the aspects of your program illustrate what the mission statement says in summary form? The advantage of developing, discussing and revisiting it as a group is that the broader the consensus about the mission statement, the greater the unity will be in carrying it out. Furthermore, discovering the strengths and weakness of the existing program in the light of the mission statement will not only clarify the task of strategic planning, but will also give impetus to making the right kinds of changes happen.

Bear in mind that changes in community needs, program realities and your capacity to respond will affect your mission statement. Organizations grow and change. A strategic planning process helps to make this change intentional. At the same time, organizational growth may suggest that it is the mission statement that needs to be changed! Either way, it is to this mission statement that we need to return over and over as we think through our program in order to determine what needs to be added, revised or retained.

3. Do a Needs Assessment

Another piece of the preparatory work necessary for strategic planning is to consider the following questions:
- Who needs you?
- How do they need you?
- How would you know?

As mentioned earlier, an educational institution cannot be all things to all people. We don't have the financial, human or physical resources or the time to accomplish everything that the church or society needs to have done. If theological education is the process of equipping men and women with the knowledge and skills needed for effective ministry, who are those men and women, and what are the ministries for which we are preparing them? If this is the context in which we intend to work, we need to know that context well.

Who is it that is being served? One would hope, for example, that a denominational program is seen by its denomination as the primary place to which their students should be sent for training. Yet there are a surprising number of schools that were founded by denominations that, for a variety of reasons, no longer send their students to their own program. If this is your reality, you need to know why not.

Even if the denomination sends its students to you, what exactly are they expecting from your training institution? Do they want Bible school teachers, pastors, church planters, Sunday school workers or Christian laity prepared for the marketplace? Do they want a two-week seminar offered in dozens of places throughout the country, or do they want multiple degree programs?

Knowing the answers to questions like these helps us focus better as we revisit our training efforts. Although there are biblical and theological foundations that should be true for all students, different ministry tasks require different kinds or levels of training. We need to know for whom we are working and for what outcomes we are expanding our training efforts.

Your training program may have a denominational name, receive significant financial support from the denomination and have a board and teaching staff that belong exclusively to churches related to the denomination. However, your students may come from a variety of churches. Perhaps many of them are not even preparing for pastoral ministry within local churches. Is it part of your "mission" to serve these students and their organizations? If not, why are you spending time, money and energy doing something that is not your mission? But if this *is* part of your mission, what are the implications for the kind of teaching staff that you need, the programs that you should be offering, and the people who sit on your governing board? Plans for responding to these strategic questions can only happen after you are clear about your constituency and their real needs.

Most Bible schools are not denominational. They were created by missionaries as independent programs, essentially working on the philosophy, "Build it, teach the Bible and students will come." Perhaps that was true, but such programs might be even better programs if they took the time to realistically assess who it is that should or could see them as their training program, while also verifying who it is that does not see them as their training program (and probably never will). It is important to determine carefully what denominations, para-church organizations, non-governmental, ethnic or linguistic groups see you as "their" program. How wide of a geographical scope do you have (or would you like to have)? Is your training focus on preparing future leaders (i.e. young people), emerging leaders or on equipping current leaders in context?

The easier part of a needs assessment comes from looking at your current students. From what churches or organizations do they come? Why did they choose you? What do they (and their leaders) expect of you? Don't just assume that you know their needs and expectations. Talk to them and their leaders about their training needs! Knowing the answers to these questions will help you to determine how well you are doing in your training efforts. An ongoing dialogue will keep you informed as to the needs of both the students and their churches or organizations. Listening to your graduates will also be of great help in informing you as to how well you have done in equipping real people for their ministries. As you perceive that you are doing well or poorly in meeting expectations, keep what is good and strengthen what isn't so good.

The harder part of a needs assessment is looking prophetically at the environment in which we work. How do social, political or economic factors affect your program? What issues directly face your students now? What are the issues for which your students need to be prepared? Some of these needs might include:

- Racial, ethnic or tribal tensions
- Being part of a minority group, especially an oppressed minority
- Injustice or corruption
- Health problems, such as malnutrition, HIV/AIDS
- War or guerrilla action
- Large numbers of refugees
- Economic difficulties, including huge gaps between the rich and the poor
- Religious conflict, such as with Islam, Hinduism or other groups
- Urban problems, such as prostitution, shack housing, violence or drugs

These needs are part of the environment in which your training program exists and into which your graduates will go. To what extent should your program be responding to these needs, and if it should, how well are you responding? The answers to these questions will help define what ought to be included in your strategic plan. (Don't forget, of course, that you cannot be all things to all people. There are hard choices to make about what can and cannot be done by you!)

It is when we have done our needs assessment well that we can more easily determine how well our curriculum has been designed. We will discuss curricular design more thoroughly in chapter 6. What is important at this point is to develop a careful profile of who your students are, including:

1. What do they know? This is more than just biblical or theological knowledge.
2. What do they know how to do? Ministry skills, study skills or life skills.
3. What kind of people are they? Character and attitudes.

We then need to describe the ministries into which our graduates will go as part of their response to the needs of the church and society, including:

1. What do they need to know in order to do these ministries?
2. What specific skills do they need as practitioners of these ministries?
3. What kind of people do they need to be in order to minister well?

If we have done a careful job of discerning the needs of students as well as the environment in which they will be ministering, then each aspect of our curriculum should describe how we intend to get them from where they are now to where they need to be.

We may conclude that we have been inadequately preparing our students for effective ministry. We also may discover that we have been recruiting the wrong people to be students, that we are teaching in the wrong places, that we have the wrong teachers or that we are using inadequate teaching methodologies. The point is: we must do some careful research in order to understand what we've done well, poorly or not at all. It is as we know these things that we can intelligently construct a strategic plan.

4. Do an Institutional Assessment – Strengths, Weaknesses and Resources

The last piece of preparatory work that needs to be done before compiling or revisiting your written strategic plan is to do an assessment of the strengths and weaknesses of the overall training program. The place to start is with the "overall" part. Every established program has some kind of visible track record. What perceptions do people have about the effects and the health of your training program? How do your teachers, staff, board and students feel? How do your graduates and the churches they serve feel about the value of the training? What does the secular community around you think about you? Look for ways for the entire academic community to affirm what it is that is done well, noting specific areas where God has blessed. Identify and celebrate these things.

It is reassuring when the wider community, both inside and outside, is in agreement about who you are and where you need to be going. To obtain a realistic understanding of the bigger picture, look for a variety of formal and informal places where you can determine which of your strengths and/or weaknesses are things that everyone seems to agree on. By asking many people simple questions about what you do well and what you don't do so well, you will be preparing the way for keeping what is good and changing what needs to be improved.

Nevertheless, a strategic planning process also needs for you to do a systematic analysis of each and every piece of your training program. The best way to do this is through organizing smaller study groups who can look at the details and make written reports of their conclusions with suggestions for change.

Each of these study groups should also begin by discussing and affirming your values. They will revisit the mission statement as this is the summary statement of what your entire program is about and serves as a reference point to help determine the effectiveness of each of the pieces of your program. A careful evaluation will then note:

1. What is very good and should be kept?
2. What needs strengthening or fixing so that it can be better?
3. What should be dropped altogether?
4. What is missing and should be added?

One of the best tools for a systematic and detailed evaluation of your program is to work through the self-study guides that are normally a part of an accreditation process (e.g. any of the eight continental agencies affiliated with the International Council for Evangelical Theological Education: www.icete_edu.org/). The following list suggests areas that need to be examined as well as some questions that might be helpful. Just remember that the phrasing of the questions is not as important as making sure that you have been thorough in looking at everything.

1. **Academic Program.**
   How strong are each of your training programs and the degrees offered through them? To what extent does the formal training that you offer accomplish in your students what your mission statement and purpose says that you intend to do? How do the standards of your training program compare with accreditation standards and/or with other programs offering comparable degrees?

2. **Character and Skill Development.**
   What evidence is there of spiritual growth and maturity in the lives of your students? To what extent is this growth the result of what you are intentionally doing to develop character? How does the environment in which you are training affect what students are really learning? How well does your field education program work? Are students showing growth in their practical ministry skills?

3. **Faculty and Staff Development.**
   How strong is your faculty (academically, teaching skills, pastoral ministry skills, other areas of practical experience, etc.)? Given that students learn most from the lives of their teachers, what are you doing to strengthen your faculty? (Peer mentoring? Coaching?) How are you doing in the development of national staff?

4. **Organizational and Administrative Leadership, Plus Support Staff.**
   How strong is your organization's leadership in terms of skills, experience, training and character? How adequate and competent is your administrative staff? Is there clarity of what needs to be done and by whom, and is there efficiency in accomplishing what needs to be done?

5. **Administrative Structures and Governance Issues.**
   How well do your administrative rules and regulations serve the purposes of your training institution? Are these written and

generally available? To what extent are you working with rules and policies that are no longer relevant to the realities of today?

6. **Board Development.**
How strong (competence of individuals, plus having the right people) is your board? How active are they, individually and as a group, in the life of the program? How adequate are your governance processes?

7. **Campus and Facilities Development, Including a Long-term Site Plan.**
How would you evaluate the adequacy of your campus facilities and equipment, including computers and Internet access? Are there ways in which you might be able to enhance your facilities by sharing them with others or by borrowing facilities that currently belong to others?

8. **Library and Information Resource Development.**
How adequate is your library collection to serve the programs that you offer? Is there a library selection policy? Has an information technology plan been developed and how are you doing in implementing this? Do your teachers and staff know how to use the research resources that you have?

9. **Students.**
How strong is your student body (academically, emotionally, spiritually, relationally)? Where are the strengths and weaknesses in your student recruitment processes? How might you discover potential students?

10. **Church and Community Relationships, Networking.**
How healthy and broad are your relationships with the churches and organizations that send (and that *don't* send) you students, staff and finances? How would you evaluate what you do in public relations?

11. **Funding Procedures and Development.**
    How strong are your finances, especially your capacity to find funds locally? How could additional sources of income be discovered? Are there ways, other than money, that people could help support your program? How adequate are your financial records, your banking systems and the staff that make this work?

5. Write / Review Your Strategic Plan

Most leadership training programs already have some kind of long-range plan. These need to be revisited at least every five years or so. If that is where you are now, involve your entire community in discussions of your values and mission, of the needs that you see and feel around you, and of your strengths and weakness as you attempt to respond to those needs with the resources that God has given you. When you have done this, it is time to draw on the conclusions and recommendations of these various working groups.

a. Review what you have discussed and concluded in the light of your core values and your mission statement. Are you doing things that really don't fit who you are? Is there a compelling reason why you should hang onto them? If not, find a gracious way to drop them.

b. Review the written needs assessment reports, as well as both the general and systematic evaluations that you have done of the various aspects of your program. As you look at your opportunities, your strengths and your weaknesses, take time to pray, dream and plan about specific ways in which you could be different. What really has been blessed and should be kept? How could these things be made even better? What is it that needs fixing? Are there new pieces that ought to be added to your program? Make lists of specific things that you should and could be doing.

c. Working from your lists, systematize and prioritize them so that each proposed change is carefully thought through. Bear in mind that doing this is not a simple process. For each item on this list, you will need to carefully and thoroughly answer three interrelated questions:

- **Outcomes.** What is it that you hope to achieve in a specific area? These are statements of faith, that is, what you believe that God wants you to be or do within the next few years.
- **Process.** How do you plan to achieve the various outcomes you propose? What will it take to get from here to there?
- **Resources.** What will it cost you, in time, people, space or finances, to be able to achieve your outcomes?

And If You Don't Have a Strategic Plan: Write One!

Following OCI's first Institute for Excellence in Nairobi in April of 1999, one of the participating programs returned home to systematically work through these questions related to strategic planning. They had been born in the apartheid days of South Africa, and as they reviewed their history they could clearly see how their values had shaped their program. Rather than consider a move to a more spacious environment outside of the city, they reaffirmed their commitment to mission in an urban context. That included ongoing development of their site plan to acquire the remaining properties so as to own the entire street where they were located. Revisiting their values, also helped them to reaffirm why it was so crucial to work at character and spiritual formation. Not only was it important to get beyond racial barriers, but also those created by denominations or gender. As they considered the needs of the city around them, it was concluded that a new initiative should be developed to prepare their students to respond to the HIV/AIDS crisis. They also considered how the students and staff could all respond compassionately to the needs of the community.

Over several years, working committees not only rewrote the school's purpose and mission statements, but the entire academic program was reconfigured. They even concluded that they needed a name change from the Evangelical Bible Seminary of Southern Africa (EBSemSA) to the Evangelical Seminary of Southern Africa (ESSA) as it made their acronym more pronounceable. (You can learn more about this creative program at: www.essa.ac.za/.)

Conclusions

A strategic plan is not a negation of our trust in God's sovereignty. As Dr John Bennett, late president of Overseas Council, said in a workshop that he presented in 1999, "Every strategic plan is a statement of faith, that is, an articulation of an unrealized future." We plan, as Nehemiah did, so that we can be faithful and effective in finishing what has been given to us to do. Our plan becomes a roadmap into the future. And as we look back, reviewing what has been accomplished will provide a basis for affirming excellence in what we have done. This will hopefully provide a great excuse for a party, to the glory of God.[1]

Discussion Questions Regarding Your Strategic Plan

1. Do you have a comprehensive strategic plan, and if so, how comfortable are you with it? If you have not done one, or are unhappy with what you have, take a deep breath and get busy on doing this right!
2. Even if you already have a formalized and published list of institutional core values, encourage individuals to make their own lists of what they think are important to your training institution. As you then meet together in smaller groups, compile your lists and reduce them to 5-10 "core values." In what way are the lists different from each other and from what exists as the official list of "core values?"
3. To what extent does your purpose or mission statement adequately describe who you are and all that you are currently trying to do? (And if you don't have one, write one!)
4. Who needs you – and how do you know? Who are all those who see you (or could see you) as "their" training program? In what ways do they need what you are trying to offer?

---

1. This chapter was presented at the ICETE meetings in the UK, August 2003; a version of this was also published as chapter 3 in *Educating for Tomorrow: Theological Leadership for the Asian Context*, eds. Manfred W Kohl and A. N. Lal Senanayake (Bangalore: SAIACS Press, 2002).

5. What is it that your training program does really well – and everybody knows it? How could you celebrate this? In what ways might you be able to make these things even better?
6. What obvious weaknesses need fixing? Which of these should be dropped altogether?
7. Do you sense opportunities for new ministries that really are a part of your mission and purpose as an organization? What needs to be done in order for these things to happen?
8. What processes or plans do you have to review and rewrite your strategic plan?

Suggestions for Further Reading

Baer, Michael R. "Strategic Planning Made Simple." *Leadership* 10 (Spring 1989): 32–33.

Banks, Robert. *Reenvisioning Theological Education: Exploring a Missional Alternative to Current Models*. Grand Rapids, MI: Eerdmans, 1999.

Dolence, Michael G., Daniel James Rowley, and Herman D. Lujan. *Working toward Strategic Change: A Step-by-Step Guide to the Planning Process*. San Francisco, CA: Jossey-Bass, 1997.

Esterline, David. "A Planning Framework for Theological Education." *Ministerial Formation* 42 (June 1998): 14–22.

Ferris, Robert W. *Renewal in Theological Education: Strategies for Change*. Wheaton, IL: Billy Graham Center, 1990.

Haworth, Jennifer Grant, and Clifton F. Conrad. *Emblems of Quality in Higher Education: Developing and Sustaining High-Quality Programs*. Boston, MA: Allyn and Bacon, 1997.

Kohl, Manfred W., and A. N. Lal Senanayake. *Educating for Tomorrow: Theological Leadership for the Asian Context*. Bangalore: SAIACS Press, 2002.

Peters, Tom. *Thriving on Chaos: Handbook for a Management Revolution*. New York, NY: Harper Collins Publishers, 1987.

Peters, Tom, and Robert H. Waterman, Jr. *In Search of Excellence: Lessons from America's Best-Run Companies*. New York, NY: Harper and Row, 1982.

Rowley, Daniel J., and Herbert Sherman. *From Strategy to Change: Implementing the Plan in Higher Education*. San Francisco, CA: Jossey-Bass, 2001.

4

Excellence in Governance

Excellent leadership training institutions are accountable to the constituencies that they serve. They are advised and governed by well-conceived and supportive advisory councils and governing boards.

In this chapter we want to examine the foundations on which theological education institutions stand. The fundamental question is one of ownership, and the key to excellence in governance is that those who are the owners must assume responsibility for what is theirs. Governance is the primary way by which training institutions are accountable for what they do, whether in the Western or non-Western world. In this chapter, I will suggest that there are three basic levels in which governance needs to be done: (1) at an authority level, by an advisory or general council representing the institution's constituency; (2) at a policy level, by a governing board or council; and (3) at an implementation level, by the institution's administrative staff team, under the leadership of the institution's principal. We will look at the responsibilities of each of these.

Are Boards Worth the Effort?

Probably so, since the written constitutions of most training programs require them to have some sort of board, council or governing body. Even so, there are lots of reasons to wonder why we should bother with boards. I have attended many board or council meetings and have found very few of them to be functional. Sometimes a board seems to be little more than a token group of national church leaders convened regularly for appearance sake, since all of the important decisions (especially those related to funding) are either made by the mission that started the school or by the school's administrative staff and faculty.

Many board members don't show up regularly for meetings anyway, and those that do come don't seem to have a clue about why they are there. In some cases, board members have to be paid honoraria and travel fees before they consider showing up. This lack of respect for boards is not surprising. In one school, the principal routinely wrote the minutes for their council meeting before the council ever met. The group knew that their meetings were pointless, although they continued to gather to listen to reports and to talk about issues before agreeing with the predetermined conclusions. I have seen people sleeping during board meetings (once even the chairman)!

Most boards seem to exist as little more than working committees, designed to help the school's administrative staff get their work done. It is amazing how much collective time can be spent by important people trying to decide whether a photocopy machine should be bought. Councils become admissions committees to consider who should or shouldn't be accepted as students into the training program. They become personnel committees to deal with salary scales and the hiring and firing of teachers. They function as grievance committees to solve relational and practical problems. They become committees for buildings and grounds, developing schedules for maintenance and debating costs for specific equipment. They become finance committees, compiling and critiquing the budget line-by-line, as well as determining how money should be handled and who should have account signatures. They become building committees to draw up site plans and to discuss the details and costs of facilities that need to be built or refurbished. All of these activities may be very helpful to a school – although it doesn't make sense to create a "board" or "governing council" made up of important church leaders or community experts just for this. Qualified volunteers could serve the same purpose and working with them would be a lot simpler.

Board meetings often aren't much fun. Relationships can be strained, such as when the leadership of sponsoring churches use the board meeting as a forum for problems that have little or nothing to do with the training program itself. Occasionally unhealthy "we-they" tensions surface between missionaries and national staff, or between the administrative leadership and the leaders of local churches. Sometimes poor dynamics arise from power struggles or cross-cultural misunderstandings between any number of different groups or individuals.

So it is worth returning to our original question: why should we bother to have a board at all? The answer lies in understanding the nature of governance: to help training programs be accountable to those whom they exist to serve as they faithfully accomplish what was intended to be accomplished. A healthy board or council provides long-term stability to training programs. However, most theological training programs lack a general understanding of governance. As their boards are neither strong nor functional they don't have a firm foundation on which to build their programs. Poor governance may be the single biggest weakness for many theological training institutions. How can we have excellence in governance?

Whose Theological Training Program or Institution Is It?

The fundamental questions of governance relate to issues of ownership. Whose school is this? With whom do we share our concerns and tell our stories? Who makes the rules that we need to follow? And who helps us to make sure that we continue to be and do what was intended?

1. Is the Government Our Owner?

Educational organizations have constitutions that require them to fulfill certain requirements before "the authorities." If they are registered or chartered, they normally need to have a board that can be held accountable for all activities of the organization. This is an important aspect of allowing our training efforts to have public credibility. However, most of us don't consider the government to be one of our "owners." The Ministry of Education (or wherever legal papers accumulate) is simply the place where documents relating to ownership are legally filed. "Trustees" who meet only to fulfill government requirements are not really representing those who are the owners.

2. Are We Our Own Owners?

Most leadership training institutions seem to function as though they were their own owners. The administrative and faculty team writes their own purpose statement and develop their own five-year plan. They make and enforce the rules regarding internal operations. Those who work for the school hire, fire and evaluate each other. They determine their own salaries and budgets, as well as assuming the responsibility of raising and administering the funds needed to function. They see accountability (explaining themselves) in three different areas:

- Validation – satisfying governmental concerns about the legality of existing as a school;
- Accreditation – satisfying peer-level institutions that what is being done is at a similar level to what everyone else is doing; and
- Community satisfaction – making the program's beneficiaries happy as students are effectively prepared for ministry.

All three of these aspects of accountability are important. Furthermore, much of the practical implementation of governance policies is a task that should be assumed by the training program's management team. However, excellent training institutions should not be their own owners. When we want to share our successes or struggles, we shouldn't primarily be talking or giving reports to ourselves.

3. *Are the Founders Our Owners?*

In places with a British colonial heritage, founders become the "company." Their appointed trustees serve for life to guarantee that the original purpose of the organization is being followed. These trustees may never meet together and are not normally involved in any of the day-to-day decisions of the organization. While there may be a managing or governing board, it is these trustees who are considered the "owners" of the company.

This isn't a structure that is helpful to most educational programs. The existence of a board of trustees who are not required to meet or to stay in touch with the activities of the school is an invitation to serious tensions with the school's board of governors (and the school itself) as the programs evolve and respond to current realities.

Neither is it helpful when founders are considered (or consider themselves) to be the owners of a training institution. It is appropriate to honor those who brought and nurtured the school into existence, but it should be clear that a leadership training program doesn't exist to benefit its historical founders in the same way that a factory exists to provide profits for its founders and stakeholders.

4. Are the Beneficiaries of the Program Our Owners?

Absolutely! The real owners of a leadership training institution are those who benefit from its program. This kind of ownership is relatively easy to visualize for institutions established, staffed and funded by a church denomination wanting to train students for its churches. This is their training effort. The denomination creates the rules, hires the teachers and staff, selects the students, approves the curriculum and budget, and provides funding for its training program.

Although things are more complicated for institutions established by organizations or individuals who wanted to create training options for the wider Christian community, the concepts are the same. All of those who benefit from its program become stakeholders in the institution. When churches or Christian organizations invest in a training institution by sending their students to be trained, by sending faculty members to teach, or by providing financing to help the school operate, they become the functional "owners" of the program. It is appropriate for each of these beneficiaries to claim that this training institution is "their" program. Founding organizations become owners of the institution in the same way, not from their historical relationship to what was done years ago, but because they continue to benefit from what is being done by and through the program. All of these owners have the right to help define the rules under which the institution should function, as they are the ones providing teachers, students and funding. It is appropriate for them to receive reports on the progress of the training efforts and to have input into the ongoing direction and functioning of what really is "their" program.

The Role of Ownership in Governance

To develop healthy governance structures, the first step for theological education institutions is to be clear on who it is that owns them. They need to understand the make-up of the broad constituency they are serving. Those who consider the institution to be "their" school need to be acknowledged, honored and listened to. This is not primarily a question of legal ownership, which is an issue that should be defined in a school's constitution. Ownership is not so much an issue of "authority over" as "responsibility for." As the owners are those who are served by the school, their own best interests are served when their training institution runs with excellence. Functional ownership will be more flexible as new "owners" opt in and non-involved former "owners" drop out. Both legal and functional ownership should be built into practical structures developed for governance. There are three basic levels in which governance needs to be done:

At an authority level, by a broad body representing the institution's entire constituency. We will refer to this as the general assembly, though it also could be seen as an advisory board or a general council.

At a policy level, by a smaller group selected for their expertise and availability to define the institutions purpose, to develop operational policy and to oversee the implementation of those policies. We will refer to this as a governing board or governing council.

At an implementation level, by those who run the training institution for the constituency within the policies established so that the institution's vision and purpose will be achieved. The institution's principal or president is responsible to see that this is done, working together with all of the school's administrative staff and faculty.

The General Assembly as an Advisory Board or Advisory Council

Denominational training programs have regularly scheduled general assemblies, composed of delegates from churches within the denomination. The agenda at the general assembly will normally include reports on the progress of the denomination's leadership training program(s). While responsibility for overseeing the health of these Bible schools and seminaries will usually be given to a smaller group selected by the assembly, this governing group will also report back to the larger assembly. The general assembly retains authority to approve all major issues concerning the school(s), such as its budget and the appointment of the principal and its governing board(s).

Non-denominational training institutions need a similar sort of general assembly. This group should be composed of all those who represent the program's "owners" and "stakeholders." They will be important leaders from churches and Christian organizations that consider this to be their school. As they are the ones providing teachers, staff, students and funding to the training program, the school must provide them with regular reports and information to help them understand the health of their institution, along with prayer and financial needs. This group should have an opportunity to discuss these issues together, as well as to give feedback regarding the success or failure of the program. This general assembly should meet at least once a year, perhaps in conjunction with major events being held at the training institution, such as graduation ceremonies or a week of special emphasis.

This representative group of owners could be called an advisory council or advisory board as they exist to give counsel and feedback more than to govern. Although the general assembly may give itself some important powers, such as approving the budget or ratifying the selection of a governing board or the school's principal, its primary focus should be on the bigger issues of results and impact, not on day-to-day operations or details. Meetings of and with this group should be designed to obtain maximum feedback concerning students and graduates, along with insights into the impact (or lack of it) that the leadership training program is having. The expertise of the group can become a forum or think-tank to help the school consider creative and new ways to do training, administration, fundraising, student recruitment, etc. These meetings can be excellent times for the leadership of the school to learn about significant trends and issues within education, the church or society in general.

This formalized advisory group may be called a board of reference, as the individuals on this board are well-known leaders whose blessing is an affirmation to the broader community of the value of the training being offered. The importance and influence of this group should not be underestimated. It is thus imperative that they feel comfortable with all aspects of what the theological training institution is trying to accomplish, as they are in a unique position to pray intelligently for the institution and to share its needs and success with the wider community.

The Governing Board

Every training program needs a governing council or board. This is a smaller group that fulfills the constitutional role of trusteeship, assuming legal responsibility for the leadership training program and its activities. It works under the broad authority of a general assembly to develop policies and rules under which a training program functions and to oversee the overall operations of the training institution.

A governing board may be called a board of directors, board of trustees or board of regents. It is the primary responsibility of a governing board or council to make sure that a training institution is doing what it is supposed to be doing. It usually is considered by the school's constitution to be the legal entity that "owns" the program (normally on behalf of the general assembly or the various organizations that the council members represent). It is ultimately accountable for all aspects and activities of the organization. The board should define and routinely affirm the basic purposes or mission of the training program, as well as its values. The board oversees the development and implementation of a strategic plan that reflects the school's mission and values as it attempts to respond to the real needs of the school's constituency, within the financial and human resources available.

A governing board or council should not have more than seven to twelve members. If it intends to hold full-day discussions, then it shouldn't need to meet together more than three times a year (two formal meetings plus participating in the annual retreat with the staff). If the board or council members live locally so that they can easily get together, they may opt to meet for half days every two to three months or so.

It is useful for theological institutions to have board members who represent a diversity of professions. That means that they should *not* all be pastors or academics. If the program's training is offered to both men and women from a variety of denominational backgrounds, council members should reflect those constituencies, that is, men and women of a variety of ages who come from different church groups. This same principle applies to denominational schools. If a significant portion of the student body, faculty or funding comes from outside the denomination, the board should have members who represent these part-owners of the program. As possible, it also can be helpful to have board members who bring specific skills, such as in human resources, business, finance, administration, media or law. Although staff members, including the principal, may serve in ex-officio ways on the governing board, they should not be members or officers of the board.

There are advantages in having a person serve as a board member long enough to thoroughly understand the history and operations of the training institution, as well as to build relationships with other board members and with staff and students. However, there also are advantages when a board member does not consider the position to be a lifelong appointment. There is wisdom in having a maximum age for service as a board member (perhaps 70-75 or so), and in allowing a board member to serve for no more than two four-to-five-year terms. This allows for renewal and the introduction of new ideas and perspectives. The board should develop procedures for the nomination and selection of new members. These could be selected (or ratified) by the general assembly in accordance with criteria that describe what qualities or experiences are wanted or required in board members.

Board members need to sense enough freedom with one another to be able to share openly and honestly as they carefully consider the various sides of complicated issues, including issues with emotional aspects. It is not helpful to push for all decisions to be made by unanimous acclamation. If people have serious reservations over a specific issue, the board can usually postpone a decision. The details of all discussion should remain confidential and when a decision is made, the board speaks with one voice. Individual members should not continue to voice their personal views outside of the board.

As the supreme governing body for a theological training institution, a governing council develops the rules or policies under which a school operates. They should not see themselves as a group of experts who exist to help the staff do its job. For example, rather than develop a budget, the governing board determines what makes a budget acceptable or unacceptable. Rather than hire and evaluate the staff and teachers, the governing board develops policies that determine what kind of teachers and administrators are (or are not) acceptable to the school. The board then monitors these policies to see that they are being appropriately implemented. The council should do this through the principal or director, who is the only person that they hire. The administrative and teaching staff report on all things to the principal, who then reports regularly to the board regarding progress, problems or issues needing discussion.

Examples of a board policy might be: "All administrative and teaching staff will have written job descriptions that include performance standards." Or: "All administrative and teaching staff will be evaluated annually according to the performance standards for their job." The board doesn't write job descriptions, performance standards or evaluation processes. These are issues of policy implementation and should be done by the school's management team. We will discuss these issues further in the next chapter. However, the board does have the responsibility to make sure that adequate job descriptions and performance standards exist for each employee of the school, that evaluations are done annually, and that all these are done in accordance with the policies that the board established.

When a board receives the report that the principal gives (which should be in their hands in a written form well in advance of the board meeting), they read it carefully (rather than having it read to them) in the light of established policies that are being implemented. A board needs to understand whether or not the leadership training program is achieving what it intends to achieve within the fundamental guidelines of what the program was created to be.

There are occasions when a governing board is required to give its blessing to decisions that are more appropriately made by others. These might include the ratification of staff or faculty appointments, approval of calendar events or approval of the budget. A token "yes" is adequate and extensive time should not be taken to systematically review what hopefully was done with competence by others – unless of course, it appears that there have been violations of board established policies. However, even then, a board shouldn't step in to do the work for the staff; it should require that those responsible redo the work. A board should use its time and expertise to discuss bigger issues, such as helping to define the kinds of teachers that are needed, or to discuss how existing faculty could be renewed or trained further. Like the general assembly, governing boards have an advisory function, and should draw on their expertise to think creatively about issues that face the institution. These could include discussions about how funding could be developed or how new students, new faculty (or even new constituencies) could be discovered.

Usually a board has a fiduciary or legal responsibility to monitor that funds are being raised and used appropriately, and with proper documentation. This is important, though it is even more important to determine whether the funds raised and expended were adequate to enable the training institution to achieve what its values and purposes state are supposed to be achieved. In all areas, a board should not become distracted by the day-to-day issues of operations. Its primary task is to guarantee that the overall training program is being effective in what it is trying to do.

Specific Responsibilities of the Board

The following list of the responsibilities of a theological education training institution board is adapted from a presentation made at an OCI Institute for Excellence in Cairo in February 2001 by Nabil Costa, the executive director of the Lebanese Society for Social Development.

1. **A board has a visionary dimension**:
    - To develop and affirm the mission of the institution (its values, purpose and statement of faith, etc.) and to keep watch over the training program or institution to ensure that this foundation is preserved.
    - To pray and dream about what the future of the program will look like. Even though most of the work in developing a strategic plan will be done by the school's management team and teaching staff, the strategic planning process is overseen by the board as it is their responsibility to make the future a reality, in accordance with the fundamental purpose and values of the program. If foundational changes are needed, it is the board that needs to affirm this.

2. **A board has an administrative and managerial dimension**:
    - To develop policies for all aspects of the operation of the training and to monitor the health of the school through the principal's reports in the light of the institution's purpose, value and policies.
    - To approve the budget (as developed in accordance with the policies that the board has established) and to ensure that proper fiscal controls are in place so that funds are appropriately used.
    - To recruit, appoint, evaluate and encourage the school's director (principal, president or chief executive officer) and new board members.
    - To evaluate its own effectiveness.

3. **A board has a public relations dimension:**
   - To know the training institution well, and be prayerfully and publicly supportive of it.
   - To help the institution to have healthy relationships with donors, churches, the community, the media, alumni and the government.
   - To assist in the finding of new donors, while being donors themselves.

4. **A board has a legal dimension:**
   - On behalf of the owners, to be responsible for all fiscal oversight and fiscal liability, as well as for the overall well-being of the ministry.

Specific Responsibilities of Board Members

Each board or council member should wholeheartedly embrace what it means to be a part of the board. Being a council member is not a position that a person takes on in order to gain prestige or to enhance his or her image in the community. Neither is it a job for which people should be paid, though if the budget allows, it is acceptable to offer reimbursement for travel. No one should accept the responsibility to serve on a governing board if he or she is not willing to regularly pray for and financially give to the institution, as well as to be informed about the program and its people through reading reports and visits, and to actively participate in all the board meetings.

Dr Manfred W. Kohl, Vice-President of International Development for Overseas Council International has shared what he calls the "Rule of Seven" at many of the OCI Institutes for Excellence. These are not rigid rules, but wise principles. According to the Rule of Seven, each board member should commit himself or herself:

1. To spend seven seconds a day in prayer for the school, its leadership and staff.
2. To spend seven minutes a week in order to read correspondence, newsletters and reports from the school; to call the principal or others to see how things are going; and as the occasion arises, to share the nature and goals of the training program with others.

3. To set aside seven hours a month to occasionally attend chapel services or staff prayer times; or to have lunch with the principal, teachers or students.
4. To give seven days a year to attend regular board meetings; to be a part of special times of prayer and planning with the board and staff.
5. To serve seven years on the board to give continuity and quality service, but then to step down in order to provide opportunity for new people with new ideas, as well as to be free to serve on the board of other organizations.
6. To spend the last seven weeks of one's term to train one's successor in order to make a smooth and uncomplicated transition; and to explain difficult or significant issues of the past.
7. To share (with the other board members) in providing 1/7 of the operating budget by personally committing financial support; by finding friends and donors interested in the ministry, and by helping to open doors and to follow-up on contacts.

The Administrative or Management Team

As we noted earlier, theological training institutions should not function as their own owners. Nevertheless, there are important governance roles that must be assumed by the school's administrative team. The training program's leadership will listen to the wisdom and advice of those important leaders who are a part of their general assembly. We need their affirmation and blessing since we are "their" training program. We want them to continue to send us students, teachers and funding. A school's administrative leadership will also respect its governing board since they have legal responsibility for all aspects of our leadership training institution. Good governance is more than a booklet containing well-constructed rules and policies. Policies need to be implemented with reports given back so that the board (and the owners) will feel satisfied that the institution is doing what it is supposed to be doing. Obviously there will need to be a management or leadership team that will assist in doing the day-to-day administrative tasks of the institution. Having a competent administrative staff team is the subject of our next chapter. However, before concluding our discussion of issues of governance, we need to consider the role and responsibility of the one person who assumes responsibility for the implementation of the vision and the policies of the training institution. This individual may be called provost, principal, CEO, chancellor, vice-chancellor, executive director or president.

The Governance Role of the Principal

In chapter 2 we discussed the qualities that need to be true in the life of any person who gives leadership to leadership training programs. We also suggested that there are four basic tasks for anyone in a position of leadership in a theological training institution: (1) A leader provides vision and a plan; (2) A leader builds, equips and encourages teams; (3) A leader teaches and master teaches; and (4) A leader represents the school publicly.

However, only one person is to be appointed as the school's leader, or principal. This is the individual hired by the governing board and ratified by the general assembly to assume total responsibility for everything that goes on within the institution. This implies that the responsibilities of the principal need to include at least the following areas:

- Strategic planning, including long-term perspectives.
- Operational and organizational planning, including staff development.
- Annual budget with regular financial reports and preparation for annual audit.
- Team development and planning with/for key staff members.
- Regular/monthly information flow to members of the board, ensuring that decisions made by the board and committees are carried out.
- Representation of the organization to the outside, including participation in international meetings.
- Ultimate responsibility for corporate identity, all publications and marketing activities.
- Preparing and attending meetings of the board and committees.

This is not a job for a perfectionist who prefers to do everything all by himself. Neither is this a job for someone whose passion is exclusively for teaching or giving pastoral care. Let teachers or preachers give their heart and soul to teaching and preaching. An effective principal, on the other hand, will need to divide his or her time into roughly three equal portions.

1. Building relationships with the governing board and the members of the general assembly. This will be both pastoral and part of the need to cast a vision. It is important to hear the heartbeat and concerns of the board and the leaders of the school's constituency. The principal will share his or her own concerns as well as what God is doing in and through the training institution. Life at a training institution will be improved if the principal invests significant time regularly with these key people.

2. Investing in the school's leadership or management team. This will involve some hands-on administration and teaching, although it also must include empowering others and master teaching in order to have a strong team that can work together in carrying out the mission of the school. We will discuss a possible structure for this leadership team in the next chapter.

3. Public relations. This may involve public speaking for fund- or friend-raising purposes in a variety of contexts, as well as holding private conversations with new and old friends. As the principal visibly represents what the school is, significant time needs to be given so that the credibility of the school can be recognized by government officials, by other training institutions and by society in general.

Conclusions

Good governance is a solid foundation for theological training institutions. It is important for the constituencies served by the training program to take real ownership of the training efforts and to develop structures that will define and preserve an institution's values and purpose. One important key to doing this with excellence is having a principal who can not only build and empower teams to implement the desires of the governing board and the general assembly, but who can inspire vision while providing pastoral care to key leaders of the school's constituency.

Discussion Questions Regarding Your Governance

1. How functional are your boards or councils?
2. Who owns you? Do they know that?

3. To what extent does your governing board function as committees, primarily doing the work of management or administrative staff? How could you help them to spend less time doing what doesn't really need to be done by them and more time doing things that are important?
4. Is your governing board or council made up of the right people? What could be done to make this a healthier governance group?

Suggestions for Further Reading

Blackman, Rachel. "Organizational Governance." *Roots* 10 (2006). An excellence resource available through Tearfund UK as part of the ROOTS series at www.tearfund.org/tilz.

Carver, John. *Boards That Make a Difference*. San Francisco, CA: Jossey-Bass, 1990.

Drucker, Peter F. *Managing the Non-Profit Organization: Principles and Practices*. New York, NY: Harper Business, 1990.

O'Connell, Brian. *The Board Member's Book: Making a Difference in Voluntary Organizations*. Washington, DC: The Foundation Center, 1985. Especially chapter 4 "The Role of the Board and Board Members" (19–32).

5

Excellence in Administration

Excellent leadership training institutions have appropriate and adequate structures that make the program work well. Good administration is done by people who have clear job descriptions and who are competent and willing to serve the teachers, staff and students so that learning occurs.

When I first went to Brazil, a Canadian colleague and I were asked by our local pastors' association to start a theological training institution. We two teachers found a U-shaped building that had formerly been a residence for Christian girls who had come to study in the city. We hired workers to remodel four of the little bedrooms into two classrooms and the caretaker's apartment into administrative office space. The dining room became our library while the remaining four little rooms on one wing housed our out-of-town students. We created our own application forms for students, as well as forms for student attendance and grades. We set up a bank account and made up our own system of finances. We bought books from what lists we could find for Brazilian publishers, and classified them for our little library. We visited local churches to promote the seminary and invited some of the local pastors to become part-time lecturers in our new school. Our curriculum was basically a compilation of what we found in other training programs across Brazil. We organized the schedules for class and chapel around when teachers could come. Although we were new teachers ourselves, we did what we could to train other teachers. In retrospect, I'm not sure that we did a bad job, but it is clear that the two of us did an awful lot of everything while knowing very little about much of it.

Most theological education programs have been started by teachers. In the initial stages of development, teachers are the ones who take on most of the administrative tasks of the new school, whether they are good at them or not. This doesn't always change with time. It is reasonable that teachers write and teach the curriculum. They are in the best position to establish academic rules and practices. Teachers should give input on student admissions, library development and facility and equipment needs. They need to have a voice in the development of a budget. But it is not usually a good idea when they also take on eternal responsibility for overseeing everything that happens on a theological school campus.

As the staffing needs of a school grow, there is a need for specialization. There are three internal areas in which excellence needs to exist in order for students to be well-equipped for ministry, only one of which is academics. Most people understand that there is an academic side to learning, for which we need books, a classroom, computers and people with teaching gifts. Yet we also need excellence in the areas of administration and fund development.

In this chapter we will look at issues of administration and structure. We will see that theological school management requires a principal who oversees three distinct areas: academic affairs, administrative affairs, and public relations and fund development. We will also look at budgets, job descriptions, hiring new people and how to strengthen the administrative staff team that we have.

The Challenge of Administration

Surprisingly few people appreciate how much can and should be done by those with administrative gifts (and not just teaching gifts) in order for a training program to function smoothly and effectively. Even fewer people understand what needs to happen for a program to have adequate financial support. Without a competent administrative team, working within well-designed administrative structures, it is impossible to have excellence in learning. Without adequate financing, neither those who teach, nor those who administrate, will be able to function at all. Learning occurs in a complicated system where many pieces need to function simultaneously.

Leadership training programs require excellence in administration. Coordinating logistics for a theological training institution can be overwhelming in programs of any size. One major reason for this is that most administrative structures, processes and rules are not the result of a carefully considered plan, designed to coherently serve the purposes of the training program. Rather, structures, practices and policies often reflect a long accumulation of responses to particular situations by individual personalities. It is common for school leadership to inherit administrative structures that are overly complicated for what needs to be done.

Simple is better. Administration is developing and coordinating a team of people who can do those specific things that need to be done to support your training program. We are not helped when we simply continue doing everything that has always been done. Neither do we build efficiency and competence into our administrative efforts when we grab whatever warm bodies might be available to do things that they may not be competent to do. We need individuals with specific skills to take on jobs worth doing as a part of making the entire educational process work with excellence.

Administration is a team effort. Perhaps the person who is most significant in presenting the public image of an institution is not the principal, but the receptionist at the entryway who personally and enthusiastically deals with visitors and phone calls. There are those who lovingly care for our property, who clean and prepare our classrooms so that teachers have chalk or whiteboard markers that work. Someone orders textbooks and other supplies six to twelve months in advance of when they are needed so that we and our students have the resources required for learning. People with special skills maintain our libraries, our building and grounds, our phone system, our photocopier and our computer equipment. Someone recruits our students and makes sure that the wrong students have not been admitted. Others help to make sure that all new students are properly oriented to our educational community. Some of our administrative team have pastoral gifts and wisdom that they use to lovingly care for students and staff. Our curricular program is monitored so that qualified teachers are available for the subjects that need to be taught, and so that classrooms are assigned with a timetable for each term. People with organizational skills coordinate and keep academic records, class syllabi, test results and credits. Administrative assistants coordinate schedules, organize meetings, prepare documents, and keep the school's correspondence up-to-date and well filed. Someone makes sure that student fees have been received, that scholarships have been appropriately administered and all bills and salaries are being paid. Internal trainers supervise, renew and equip all of us for a variety of tasks. All of these describe administrative jobs, most of which shouldn't be done by people who only have teaching gifts – even in small training efforts.

We are part of an environment in which learning happens. The students and the community around us watch how people serve God with joy and competence – or not. The way that faculty, administrators and staff relate to each another and to students is a powerful lesson about the body of Christ. For good or bad, what we do and who we are in community will be replicated in the churches and ministries of our students when they graduate.

Appropriate Administrative Structures

Somebody has to be in charge. As we noted in the last chapter, this person, whether called principal, president, provost, vice-chancellor or chief executive officer, is the one who has been selected and empowered by the school's governing body to implement policies that will help the training institution accomplish what it is supposed to accomplish. To do this, one of his or her primary responsibilities will be to develop, train and supervise a team for three different, but interrelated, areas in which excellence needs to exist:

- Academic affairs.
- Administrative affairs.
- Public relations and fund development.

In one sense, all of these areas involve administration as they are part of the overall package of logistics that makes a training program work. Yet as they involve distinct aspects of a training program, each should be treated separately and should be led by someone designated to provide leadership over that particular area. Depending on the size of the training program, these might not need to be full-time administrators. These administrative leaders could be given a variety of titles, such as coordinators, directors, deans or vice-presidents. Given the different skills involved, each coordinator should have responsibility for only one of these three areas. However, all three work closely together under the leadership of the school's principal, knowing that there is a significant and dynamic inter-relationship among areas.

1. Academic Affairs

This may be the area that is easiest to conceptualize. We know that competent teachers need to be found, trained and renewed. A contextualized program of study to equip students for ministry should exist. Teaching outcomes and methodologies must be defined for all courses with syllabi kept and monitored to ensure quality in each course offered. Field education and character development need to be structured into the overall teaching program. A dean of students may be appointed to the academic affairs team to help oversee the spiritual growth of students. A librarian may also become part of this academic team, given the importance of books and electronic resources for learning. Policies will be needed for grading, along with the careful keeping of academic records. Someone needs to develop a timetable for classes and a schedule for the use of classrooms.

The Role of an Academic Vice-President or Dean

An academic dean or a coordinator for academic issues has the primary responsibility to oversee the development and teaching of the school's curriculum. Academic deans need organizational and relational skills, along with basic competence and experience as educators. Their task is to build a strong teaching team that is committed to a contextualized curriculum so that the organization can do what it intends to do in equipping people for ministry. Academic deans should have a clear understanding of the strengths and weaknesses of their training efforts. They function less as pioneers of new efforts than as managers of people doing a variety of interrelated tasks. If they are successful and fair in their leadership, everyone will have a sense that their task was done by all of them. The responsibilities of an academic dean include at least these seven important elements:

1. **Curriculum development**. The academic dean should oversee an ongoing process of evaluation and review of the curriculum to insure its relevance. Teachers need to understand the role that each of them has in making the curriculum effective.
2. **Consensus concerning vision**. Faculty are a bit like cats in that they are very difficult to herd. A good dean knows how to build consensus so that there will be a common sense of what everyone is trying to do. Relationships are important and decisions need to

be made together. Jeanne P. McLean wrote that the dean serves as "facilitator, negotiator, and guide. Deans exercise leadership by enabling others to participate in governance and to achieve their common goals."[1]

3. **Faculty development**. The dean should develop a regular system of student and colleague feedback to help teachers know how to teach better. Faculty should be helped and encouraged to participate in seminars or professional workshops to improve their skills and to build relationships with colleagues. The dean should coordinate efforts to allow faculty to obtain advanced formal training.

4. **Student development**. The academic dean should oversee both the dean of students and the field education program. Student progress, issues and problems should be known and appropriately provided for.

5. **Problem solving and conflict resolution**. The academic dean becomes a court of appeals for most academic issues, including requests for exceptions to rules and disciplinary problems. The dean serves as mediator for conflicts that arise between faculty and students or among staff members.

6. **Budget and program development**. The academic dean is responsible for presenting what is needed for the healthy functioning of the academic program in personnel, equipment and finances.

7. **Influence and relationships**. The academic dean represents the academic team and should maintain close relationships with the leadership of the overall training program and its governing body. When approvals are needed, the academic dean defends the process and the conclusions.

2. Administrative Affairs

There are many details involved in running a theological training program. When the little things are not taken care of by people who are good at taking care of details, the effects are felt by everyone. In a February 2006 letter to

---

1. Jeanne P. McLean, *Leading from the Center: The Emerging Role of the Chief Academic Officer in Theological Schools* (Atlanta, GA: Scholars Press, 1999), 74.

mission leaders, SIM's International Director, Malcolm McGregor, noted that the lack of good administrative support was one of the issues that most threatened the health and welfare of leaders. He cited a situation with one individual: "He has a huge heart and vision for the work going on . . . yet is weighed down due to a lack of administrative support. It prevents him engaging with ministry and strategic issues, it keeps him from being out among his team and it draws energy out of him – yet he is a gifted leader."

There are at least seven broad areas where administration needs to happen in order for your leadership training program to work well:

1. **Registrar and admissions** – to ensure that the right people are admitted to the program and that their documents show how they are moving toward graduation in their program of study.
2. **Personal assistants and secretarial help** – to ensure that handouts or exams are ready for teachers, that conferences or special guests are cared for, that student and class records are carefully maintained, that government paperwork is up-to-date, and that all correspondence is responded to from potential students, alumni, churches, donors and others.
3. **Purchasing** – to ensure that the school has the equipment and the day-to-day supplies and resources it needs, including textbooks, whiteboard pens, paper, file folders, etc.
4. **Maintenance of equipment** – to ensure that things work, like telephones, computers, Internet connections, the photocopy machine and whatever vehicles you might have.
5. **Maintenance of buildings and property** – to ensure that classrooms, offices, the library and the chapel are all properly cleaned and cared for, that lights have light bulbs that work, that student desks or chairs are usable, and that the campus is neat and secure.
6. **Personnel** – to ensure that people are properly hired, that personnel records are maintained, and that everyone has an up-to-date written job description with a clearly defined salary and benefits package for each position.
7. **Finances** – to ensure that student fees and donations are receipted and deposited properly, that bills and salaries are paid, including

social obligations required by governments for all employees; that proper records exist for budgets and audits. A lack of trust over the use of funds can become fatal for a training program.

The Role of an Administrative Vice-President

The business world may call its director of administration a "chief operating officer" as he or she has the responsibility to oversee the details involved in making the operations work. Although administrative officers do not need experience or competence as educators, for our purposes, they need good organizational and relational skills along with a thorough commitment to theological education. Their task is to build, equip and empower a strong administrative team that actually will cover all three areas in which excellence is required for the training program: academics, public relations/ fundraising, and general administration. Like academic deans, they need to be skilled managers of people who are working in a complex variety of tasks.

The director or vice-president of administration will need to understand both the big and little pieces of the school's educational process. There are lots of things that cry daily for someone's attention. These may include discovering that there is not enough sugar for tea for students and faculty after today's chapel services, arranging for someone to be at the airport "right now" to meet a visiting lecturer, dealing with a student's immediate financial crisis or finding a car and a driver to take a staff member to the hospital. All of these are important, but an administrative officer will know how to balance immediate crises with long-range issues that also need attention and finances, such as projects for equipment purchase, personnel development or preventative maintenance for campus buildings.

3. Public Relations and Fund Development

Given that most organizations don't run very well without funding, it is important to remember that public relations and fund development is a part of the overall administrative task of any training institution. Theological training institutions need to handle financial issues with transparency and wisdom. The development of a budget is a group exercise, while the actual management of funds belongs to the administrative affairs team. However, someone has to take on the responsibility of finding the funds that an institution needs. This area of administration combines a communications task of sharing the vision, and stories of God at work with a fundraising task of finding those who are willing to invest in leadership training. The concept of public relations requires good relationships with the churches who send students, faculty and staff – and funding. It also involves ongoing relationships with the school's graduates, as well as with businesses, foundations, organizations and key individuals. For the educational ministry of the school to exist, this part of the school's administrative team needs to find creative ways to share the success and needs of the training program with those who believe in the value of the program.

The Role of a Vice-President for Public Relations and Fund Development

OCI's Dr Manfred W. Kohl refers to this as a Director of Communications and Fundraising. The person who gives leadership to this area does not need educational experience or competence, although he or she will need a deep commitment to theological education. There also may not be a need for expertise in either financial management or administrative coordination. But these leaders need superb relational and communications skills. Their task is to find, equip and manage a team that can build relationships and share information on behalf of the training program with alumni, churches, the business community and government authorities. They will need to understand the strengths and weaknesses of their theological training program and will know how to communicate this in appropriate ways to those to whom the school matters (or should matter). They know how to ask for help, and they regularly report back to those who are a part of the school's support team. In chapter 10 we will discuss in more detail ideas as to how funding can and should be developed.

Developing a Budget

Why do we even need a budget? For many schools the continuing shortage of funds means that we use what little we have for whatever cries the loudest.

One of the most important reasons for developing a budget is that it forces us to prioritize what we are doing. It is good to make prayerful choices about how we use what we have, and as we put these choices in written form, we have a financial plan that can be evaluated. We will affirm together those important things that we would like to be able to do, *if only* we could find the resources to do them. Our budget becomes part of our vision as we share what we see as legitimate needs with those who join us in praying for God's provision, while also considering if they could help us financially.

A budget helps us to live as stewards. All that we have has been given to us by God (Ps 24:1), and we are not free to simply spend it for what makes the most noise. Our budget helps us exercise self-control to spend what we have for that for which it was intended. This is especially important in maintaining our credibility with donors, as it is almost never a wise decision to use funds for things *other* than that for what they were given.

The development of a budget is ultimately the responsibility of a school's principal, though in reality many people contribute to it. A budget usually needs approval by the governing board and possibly by the general assembly. Budgets need to be comprehensive, bearing in mind all three of the administrative areas of a school's functioning. Thus money will need to be allocated for the academic program (salaries and benefits, library collection, teaching equipment and supplies), for administration (salaries and benefits, maintenance, communications, buildings and grounds, etc.) and for fundraising and public relations (salaries and benefits, travel costs, publications and communications, etc.). One of the best ways to develop a budget is to look at what was actually spent in any given year, then make projections of needs for the coming year. Budgets also include reflection on possible income sources. We will discuss issues of fundraising further in chapter 10.

How Much Administrative Staff Is Too Much?

Unless your training institution is blessed with incredibly generous levels of financing, there are limits to how many people you should hire as teachers or for administrative jobs. It is easy to find tasks for which we would like to have workers, but the reality is that there can be too many workers for too few students. Most programs cannot afford to have seven teachers for only twenty students. It isn't reasonable to maintain a vehicle and a driver just for the principal. It is not likely to be cost-efficient to run a full kitchen when only lunch (and perhaps tea) is served to less than one hundred students and staff.

If the campus is large or if a large number of different training program options are offered, it is easy to acquire a large number of security guards, maintenance personnel, teachers and support staff. But a program should *never* have more employees than students. For example, while the accreditation standards for the Middle East Association for Theological Education (MEATE) require that "the teaching staff must be of sufficient number to support the educational program effectively,"[2] they assume that most programs will have more than one student studying under each teacher. MEATE suggests that there should be "at least one teacher for every fifteen students."[3] For master's- or doctoral-level programs, the teacher-student ratio may need to be less, such as one teacher for each ten students. In addition, no program should need more than two support and supervisory staff for each teacher. That suggests an overall ratio of not more than one staff member for every three to four students. If this doesn't describe your ratios, either you need a whole lot more students, or you are on a campus that is too big or too costly, or you are trying to do more than really needs to be done by you!

Caution: Don't Take on Unnecessary Administration!

Many training institutions were begun by people with visions that included far more than just training. For example, the leader of a missions training program may also want to start new churches or to send out and maintain its own graduates as missionaries. Or the leader of a theological training institution may want to use the campus and its administrative resources, including students and faculty, to respond to community needs. Thus in addition to managing its training program, an institution may also be taking on the coordination of projects in areas of community health, community development or working with HIV-AIDS and community-based orphan care. These projects are then managed by the school's staff, funds are raised and administered through the school's financial system, and their facilities may house the volunteer teams who come to work with the projects.

---

2. "Teaching Staff" in MEATE's Accreditation Manual, Point 2.1.1. This document is available from the Middle Eastern Association for Theological Education, MEATE, P.O. Box 166876, Achrafieh, Beirut, Lebanon, www.meate.org.

3. MEATE Accreditation Manual, Point 2.1.2.

Outreach and caring for needy people are valid activities in the kingdom of God. However, they can become distractions from our training efforts. They can even become something bigger than the training institution. We don't need the tail to wag the dog. If our purpose is to equip leaders for ministry, it is better to find ways to work as friends and partners in parallel universes. If your campus has extra space, an office or building could be given to a mission agency organized to send and support missionaries or new church planters. Or space could be given (or rented) to an agency created to coordinate volunteers as they work with community health projects or respond to the needs of HIV-AIDS orphans. While your students (and staff) will benefit by cooperating with projects like this as part of their field education, it is better for these projects to function independently of the training program. Coordinating volunteers or managing projects like these is probably not the core purpose of your training institution. So these things should not become the responsibility or focus of the school's leadership team or its fundraising efforts. Outreach projects need their own budgets, governing boards and administrative and staff teams.

Job Descriptions

Every person who works for a theological education training institution should have his or her own written job description, detailing what he or she is expected to be and do and how this fits into the overall mission of the school. People need a description of the character and job performance standards required and to whom they are to be accountable. A good job description will serve as the basis for doing evaluations as well as a guide for staff development, suggesting training that might be required before or after taking the job.

According to Peter Wiwcharuck, the following information should be provided on every job description:
- The title of the job, and the date when this version of the job description was written.
- The primary objective of the overall organization.
- The primary objective of this particular position (i.e. a job summary as well as where this particular person fits into the total organizational chart of the organization).

- The lines, details and limitations of the authority of the position.
- The details of each activity to be done.[4]

A well-written job description will serve as a tool for hiring people, allowing them to see what authority and responsibilities would be involved in the position they are considering. Once they accept the job, it then becomes a kind of contract, indicating their agreement to do what the school expects from them.

Job descriptions should be written for the position and not around the gifts of a particular individual. Nevertheless, it is good to leave space for a person to be able to develop a job within his or her unique personality and experience. Job descriptions should be written initially by a school's leadership, given their knowledge of what needs to be done. However, all job descriptions should be reviewed at least once a year. The best person to rewrite a job description is the person doing the job, as he or she is aware of what needs to be done and how. Any changes to a job description need to be approved by one's supervisor. While both the supervisor and the employee need copies of what has been agreed upon, a master copy of each new version should be kept by the program's personnel department.

Hiring New People

The first step in hiring new staff is to know exactly what it is that we are looking for. A variety of people can give their input as we are a community working together to equip people for ministry. Do we really need a new person? If so, we need to carefully define the job that needs to be done, along with the skills, character and personality that will be needed to get the job done. Even when we are adding people to take us into new areas, we shouldn't be reshaping and complicating our organizational chart. We are working together to achieve a common purpose. All staff, new and old, need to fit in as part of our community and as part of the collective effort to accomplish what we intend to accomplish.

Your training program may have a personnel committee that oversees the hiring process. Academic deans and faculty usually want to give input into the

---

4. Peter Wiwcharuck, *Building Effective Leadership: A Guide to Christian and Professional Management* (Three Hills, Alberta: International Christian Leadership Development Foundation, 1987), 175–176.

kinds of teaching staff that they need. A librarian will want to be a part of the hire of those who will work in the library. Governing boards or sponsoring churches may want to give their suggestions regarding people that might be helpful to you. However, staff hiring is ultimately the responsibility of the director or principal of the training program.

An individual or a search committee should only begin to look for people with the skills, experience, personality, character and vision that we want when we have developed a clear job description and when we have defined the salary benefits that will go with the job. Most governments have laws that stipulate how jobs may be filled. We may need to follow a timetable as we advertise the position publicly, receive written applications from potential employees, and conduct formal interviews. However, this does not restrict us from soliciting applications from qualified people that we already know would fit the job well.

Any job application should include at least the following information: Contact information, family status, academic records, previous employment, church affiliation and involvement, adherence to the school's statement of faith and code of conduct, and proof of specific skills related to the job position. One useful question to ask is: "Why would you like to have this job position with us?" We need staff members who not only have competence, but who believe in what we are trying to do.

From the applications that you receive, determine who is the most likely candidate. Holding interviews allows you to sense a person's spiritual commitment and compatibility with the school's mission and ethos. Besides determining their competence to do the job, we should listen for their passion and dreams. Is this the kind of person that we want to have as part of our team? Only consider one person at a time, and carry the process to its conclusion before moving on to the next name on the list. That doesn't mean that you can't look for potential new faculty members, but it does suggest that it is not wise to seriously consider three individuals as final candidates for the same NT position at the same time.

One needs to be cautious before simply hiring new people for jobs that aren't being done (or aren't being done well). As you look at specific cases, you may conclude that you have been putting energy into something that really doesn't need to be done at all or that doesn't need so many people to do it. You may be better off dropping the project than hiring new people.

Alternatively, you may conclude that existing administrative support has been done so poorly that you have made the job almost impossible to do. Don't hire new staff to compensate for interpersonal conflicts or someone's incompetence. In any of these scenarios, one first needs to deal with the issues involved: incompetence, conflict resolution or administrative support for projects. Hiring new people will not solve most of our problems.

Strengthening the Administrative Staff Team That We Have

It is much better to equip, encourage and empower the staff members that we have than to constantly be looking for new people. The most important administrative goal is to have a team of emotionally healthy people competently doing what needs to be done. People have a right to be given respect for who they are. We need to provide them with adequate health care and salary benefits that are appropriate for their level of training and for the jobs that they are doing.

One way of equipping others is to give them regular and honest feedback on what they are doing. Job appraisals, drawing on the job descriptions of each person, should be done for everyone. This helps us maintain high standards in fulfilling the mission of the school. It also allows problems to surface. We may discover that some of our colleagues are being asked to do things for which they are capable, but for which they have not been adequately trained. Alternatively, we may see where they are not doing what they might be best at, while trying to do things that we have asked them to do, but which someone more qualified could have done a lot better. Part of the problem of "filling holes" with whatever warm bodies we can find is that we burn our people out, while simultaneously perpetuating mediocrity. Clear job descriptions and regular evaluations can help prevent this.

Helping one another to be competent is an important commitment that we make to those who work with and for us. Staff development must be an important part of our administrative plan. The best teachers are those who keep on learning. The same principle is true of administrative staff members. Peter Drucker commented that "Burnout, much of the time, is a cop-out for being bored."⁵ We won't encourage excellence if our teachers and administrative staff are bored and locked into routine. We need to be a community with a culture that constantly tries to discover how to help each other to improve. We will look further at issues of evaluation and renewal in chapter 12.

We also need to provide encouragement and pastoral care. All people go through times of emotional, physical or spiritual crises. These inevitably affect the way that they do their jobs. So to what extent are these factors only temporarily causing a person to do a poor job? Being an administrator of people means that we will know how to be supportive of those who are going through difficult times.

Conclusions

There are many tasks that need to be done with competence for our training efforts to function with excellence. Teachers can happily serve with peace of mind as they know that effective structural and administrative procedures are in place. We need to be able to trust the abilities and character that exists in those that work with us and around us. Excellence in administration involves not only caring for the many details of what we are trying to do. It also includes the management of people who make the program work. Who we are as a learning community will be a major part of shaping how our students view the churches that they will plant and serve.

Discussion Questions Regarding Your Administration

1. What is the history behind your administrative structures?
2. Make a long list of every detail that needs to be done well in order for your training program to function well. Who has responsibility for making sure that these details are taken care of?
3. Draw up (or review) your flow chart of how people relate to each other in doing what needs to be done. Who relates to whom? How do they all relate to each other?

---

5. Peter Drucker, *Managing the Non-Profit Organization* (New York, NY: Harper Business, 1990), 197.

4. Does every person working with your training program have a written job description? Examine your own job description and discuss how adequate this is. How could this be improved?
5. How complicated are your administrative structures? Is there a better way to organize the way things are done?
6. Do you have more people doing administrative jobs than is justified by the number of students? How can you change what needs to change?
7. How are you structured to equip and care for the people who are currently a part of your administrative and teaching team?

Suggestions for Further Reading

Bright, David F., and Mary P. Richards. *The Academic Deanship: Individual Careers and Institutional Roles*. San Francisco, CA: Jossey-Bass, 2001.

Drucker, Peter. *Managing the Non-Profit Organization*. New York, NY: Harper Business, 1990.

Haworth, Jennifer Grant, and Clifton F. Conrad. *Emblems of Quality in Higher Education: Developing and Sustaining High-Quality Programs*. Needham Heights, MA: Allyn and Bacon, 1997.

Langford, David P., and Barbara A. Cleary. *Orchestrating Learning with Quality*. Milwaukee, WI: ASQC Quality Press, 1995.

McLean, Jeanne P. *Leading from the Center: The Emerging Role of the Chief Academic Office in Theological Schools*. Atlanta, GA: Scholars Press, 1999.

Wiwcharuck, Peter. *Building Effective Leadership: A Guide to Christian and Professional Management*. Three Hills, Alberta: International Christian Leadership Development Foundation, 1987.

Wolverton, Mimi, Walter H. Gmelch, Joni Montez, and Charles T. Nies. *The Changing Nature of the Academic Deanship*. ASHE-ERIC Higher Education Report, Vol. 28, no. 1. San Francisco, CA: Jossey-Bass, 2001.

6

Excellence in Curriculum

There is no perfect curriculum where "one size fits all." An excellent program equips specific students for ministry within a specific context. Its curriculum is creatively taught by teachers whose lives illustrate what they are saying.

One can hear a lack of popular enthusiasm for leadership training programs among those who feel that theological education doesn't effectively equip its graduates with theory, biblical foundations and practice for life or ministry. Is the problem with the curriculum? Five problem areas all relate to curriculum.

1. Is our curriculum incapable of doing intentional character development or teaching spiritual disciplines? Unfortunately, there is a clear lack of character in some of those who hold diplomas from Bible schools and theological seminaries.

2. Does our curriculum dampen students' passion for reaching the lost and thus hinder those who give leadership to the churches that are growing the fastest? One of the speakers at the Global Consultation on World Evangelization (GCOWE) in Pretoria in July of 1997 said that theological schools are one of the biggest obstacles to world evangelism.

3. Is a traditional curriculum capable of imparting the practical pastoral and leadership skills that people need for ministry?

4. Does our curriculum prepare graduates to deal with issues, such as political corruption, ethnic genocide and apartheid, or the disparity between rich and poor? There is a perception of a lack of relevance between what is taught and the world in which we live.

5. Are there simply better ways to train leaders? Is our curriculum based on teaching methodologies that are no longer valid? Have we failed to learn from what others are doing?

It is important to note those training institutions that are producing excellent graduates. It is also reassuring to hear a call to renewal by those who give accreditation to training programs.[1] Yet we are right to be concerned if we suspect that we may be teaching the wrong things in the wrong ways to the wrong people. How can we evaluate our own curriculum and to what extent is this at the core of our problems?

In this chapter we will consider the nature of curriculum. We will see that God has his own curriculum to mold chosen and gifted people for holy living and loving service using training that is informal, non-formal and formal. A good curricular plan understands the part of the task that is ours to do. It builds on the experience and knowledge that our students already have and equips them for the ministries to which God has called them. We will discuss issues of character development, course design and how to use and evaluate curricular materials.

What Is Curriculum?

The term curriculum has its origins in the Latin word *currere*, which means "to run a race." The race is not primarily that of an intensive weekend seminar or an exhausting semester, but of life! Note that a *Curriculum Vita*, our CV, describes everything of importance to us (so far) in our existence: birth, marriage, children, education, work experiences, honors received, etc.

Our personal "curriculum" is a summary, or *résumé*, of what has happened in and through us because of all that has happened around us. This is profoundly theological. For those who have been adopted as God's children, he has a wonderful plan for our lives. Paul declares, "We know that in all things God works for the good of those who love him, who have been called according to his purpose" (Rom 8:28). Paul affirmed, "It is God who *works in you* to will and to act according to his good purpose" (Phil 2:13). Paul had confidence in what would be happening with his friends in Philippi,

---

1. E.g. the 1995 ICETE Manifesto, http://www.theoledafrica.org /ICETE/ICETE Manifesto.asp.

"that he who began a good *work in you* will carry it on to completion until the day of Christ Jesus" (Phil 1:6). We are participating in a lifelong curriculum that God is working out in us.

For theological education training programs, curriculum can be understood in several different ways:

- As a list of subjects offered.
- As an instructional plan for any one of those subjects, using a variety of learning experiences to lead a person towards achieving certain planned outcomes.
- As a programmed piece of instruction for a specific course (such as curriculum for teaching computer skills, leadership management, or a 13-week series of Sunday School lessons).
- As the overall effects of an entire educational package.

In considering the impact of a training institution, it is this latter piece that is most important. The curriculum includes everything we do that contributes to the growth of students. Dr Victor Cole has written that a curriculum is "the totality of the process of an educational plan of action."[2] Curricular plans are how we structure the entire educational process. There are two basic pieces to any curricular plan:

1. **Content to be taught**. "You need to learn *this*."
2. **Someone to be equipped in character and for ministry**. "*You* need to learn this."

Bible schools have often emphasized one of these at the expense of the other. Content can become a sacred box of accumulated wisdom or traditions to be poured into a student's head, irrespective of how useful the material may be for that student. Alternatively, focusing only on an individual's equipping or formation may reduce training to the mastery of techniques, with little self-understanding and minimal biblical or historical foundations on which to stand. Both content and practice are important.

However, while a really good teacher can help his or her students to achieve high marks on content exams and (within the capacity and abilities of the student) to achieve much in skill development, no human teacher can

---

2. Victor Cole, *Training of the Ministry* (Bangalore: Theological Book Trust, 2001), 38.

change the human heart or ultimately re-shape the mind. Transformation is the work of God.

God's Curricular Plan

In organizing a curricular plan for adult learners, we must become aware of our role within God's lifelong curriculum for the student. We need to know what God has already been doing in a person's life and then find appropriate ways to facilitate the continuing process of learning and growing towards maturity. Every individual's CV should show the good works that have been done while he or she was being conformed to the image of Jesus. God's final exam is pass-fail, and those who succeed will hear, "Well done, good and faithful servant!" There are five biblical passages that allow us to see some of the principles of God's curricular plan.

1. God Is Already at Work (Rom 12:1–2)

We enroll in God's educational plan when we offer ourselves to him as living sacrifices, accepting by faith with gratefulness what he has done for us and in us. We can't change ourselves from bad to good, but we can be transformed and renewed in order to know God and his will. Yet we continue to live within a specific context. Most of what we know – our worldview, core values, and basic behaviors (including a lot of sinful habits) – has come from our environment. As God works in us, it is important to become aware of both the positive and negative effects that our culture has on us so that we can resist continuing to be "conformed to this world."

2. Learning Is Worth the Effort (Prov 2:1–6)

Although wisdom is a gift from God, there are things that we, as God's students, are to do to acquire wisdom and understanding. We need to come to his word with a heart inclined to accept it and with a mind ready to remember it. Like all good students, we are to be active learners asking questions and speaking up when we don't understand. Learning requires research and effort, but it is motivated by the value of the result: a knowledge of God.

3. Training Is for Obedience (Matt 28:18–20)

The Great Commission concludes: "Teaching them to obey all that I have commanded you." This suggests two important aspects of God's curriculum: (1) Those who are to be taught include *all* those who have been evangelized and baptized. (2) What matters is not what we know or know how to do, but obedience to all that Jesus commanded. Most of our training programs don't know how to design a curriculum that teaches obedience. We do better at giving quizzes, tests and projects.

4. Truth Is to Be Taught, Modeled and Put into Practice (2 Tim 2:2; 3:10–17)

In God's curriculum, what we learn from others is to be re-taught. The Scriptures are foundational to lead us to salvation and equip us for ministry. That God's Word is useful for "teaching, rebuking, correcting and training in righteousness" suggests both a positive and a negative aspect to God's educational process. Learning involves removing bad thinking and wrong doctrine (correction) as well as understanding what is right (teaching). Learning to live and to minister requires correcting bad behavior and practice (rebuking), while seeing positive models and receiving encouragement (training in righteousness). Models are an important part of God's educational plan. Timothy could continue in what he had learned because he knew what both content and practice looked like in the lives of those from whom he had learned. Timothy had observed Paul's way of life, his purpose, faith, patience, love, endurance, persecutions and sufferings. God's intent is that his students will be mature and thoroughly equipped for every good work through their study of his Word and from the models of their teachers.

5. Everyone Is to Be Equipped to Use Their Gifts (Eph 4:7, 11–16)

It is only as each part of the body of Christ does its work that the whole body, which is joined and held together by every supporting ligament, is able to grow and build itself up in love. All of God's people are gifted, though not everyone has the same gifts. The methodology of God's curriculum is for leaders to learn how to equip others to do the work so that everyone is adequately equipped to use the gifts that he or she has.

What Curriculum Is Fundamentally Not

1. Curriculum Is Not a Package to Be Passed On

Theological training is not passing on the exact same package that we were given. We tend to not only teach in the *way* that we were taught, but to teach exactly *what* it was that we were taught. It is not appropriate to simply re-teach the same class notes and textbooks that have always been used, especially when those textbooks weren't written for the environment and needs of the student we are teaching. We need to critically reflect on whether what we are doing is biblical, relevant to the lives of our students and effective in equipping them for their own ministries.

2. Curriculum Is Not a Monastic Experience

A curriculum is not something to be absorbed over three to four years while living on or near a campus with its dormitories, resident scholars, a library and impressive buildings. Some graduates seem to have acquired their credentials by merely spending time in the neighborhood. They have "had" four years of theology as all can see by the certificate or diploma hanging prominently on their wall. Yet little learning occurred if their lives didn't change or if they can't remember much of what they studied.

3. Curriculum Is Not Preparing a Few, Especially for the Wrong Things

A curricular plan is not a pathway for graduates to become an elite group of special people called to bless others through their efforts. We have failed if our graduates (and their churches) feel that they are to become the paid professionals who should do, on behalf of their churches, all of the church's visitation, pastoral care, evangelism, social outreach and administration. We have also failed if our training efforts have produced performers who present polished and entertaining worship services each week for the "masses" who come to pray and pay for those who do everything for them and for their pleasure.

How People Learn

A good curriculum equips real people for real ministries. There is no perfect global curriculum taught by the world's greatest teachers or a single educational package that can be used everywhere with anyone. One size does not fit all. People learn in a variety of settings and in a variety of ways. As all of our students are already enrolled in God's educational program, we need to be aware of where they are in their journeys with God. Developing curricula requires us to understand something of the environment in which people learn, so that we can more adequately prepare a curricular plan to equip our students.

People Learn Informally

Most of anything significant that any of us have learned probably did not come from formal education. We continue to be shaped by the world around us. That includes both the good and bad of what we've absorbed from home, the neighborhood, church, friends and work. We have "learned" how and what to see, and how to interpret those things. We probably non-critically reflect the values, behavior and worldview of our cultural and natural heritage. Like those before us, we're selfish by nature and we've learned how to be manipulative. We know how to create problems and avoid conflict. While most of us want to change so that we can live differently, our self-help plans will fail since only God can transform a person from within. We need God's Holy Spirit to be at work in us in the context of healthy Christian communities.

A good curricular plan recognizes the importance of the environment and the community in learning. Who we are and what we do as a learning community will have the greatest influence on what and how our students actually learn from us. We will want to help them develop a critical self-understanding of themselves and their backgrounds. We will use small groups to help people help each other to grow. We will give good advice as we encourage one another. We will also consciously identify good and bad models that will encourage our students to live in a way that glorifies God.

People Learn Non-Formally

We have all learned from small groups, seminars or workshops. Although you received no academic credit for years in Sunday school, hopefully you learned something about God! You may have been part of a Bible study group, or you attended a weekend workshop on marriage enrichment or on missions or on how to share your faith. Perhaps you have taken a short course to learn how to use a computer program, to fix truck engines or to scuba dive. Maybe you read a book about HIV-AIDS. Many people are required to do in-service training. Theological education by extension courses offer in-service training for those who are doing ministry to do it better. Some people have been apprenticed to learn specific skills. Perhaps you have been mentored by an older person. All of these are non-formal ways to learn. Adults appreciate training to help them learn things they want to learn.

A good curricular plan will include specific topics that people know they need to acquire. For example, a course on pastoral ministry should functionally be a whole series of seminars on skills that a pastor will need to have. Some of these could be offered as continuing education seminars for graduates or for Christian leaders in the area. The skills and wisdom of existing church leaders could be drawn on for apprenticeships or programs of mentoring for individual students.

People Learn Formally

When people think of "learning," they normally think of schools and campuses. Most people have spent years in institutional learning environments. In formal study, the curriculum is a package of explicit content and skills to be taught in a defined sequence. There are requirements for entry and standards to be met in order for a student to receive a diploma or degree. Students may study full-time during the day or evening, or part-time through modular study in a variety of locations or on campus during weekends or holiday times. Formal study can include programs for education by extension or study done by correspondence or through the Internet.

Theological education training programs are examples of formal learning. A good curricular plan will use the time it has available for formal study with wisdom. There are only so many courses that can be included in a three to four-year program. Not everything that has ever been taught needs to be taught by you. Furthermore, every instructor needs to remember that students will learn more from the informal or non-formal training than from what happens in a formal class setting. That doesn't minimize the importance of formal classes, but it should help us teach with realism and humility.

What a Curricular Plan Needs to Be

Even the best seminary cannot make people into pastors or evangelists. But it can take those who have pastoral or teaching gifts and help them to pastor or teach better. Equipping students for ministry is a complicated task, as we work with students who come with a variety of gifts, abilities, experience and training. They have differing interests, motivations and attitudes and learn in different ways, especially at different ages. Equipping students for ministry is further complicated by the relatively small amount of time we have to work with, coupled with the inadequacies of our resources and the limitations of our teaching team. Nevertheless, it isn't our task to do everything, only to participate well in what God is already doing in our students. A curricular plan is how we structure our part of this educational process.

A curricular plan needs to be built on four basic questions:

1. What Is the Task That Is Ours to Do?

The primary educational goal of a theological education curriculum should be to equip real people for real ministry. But there are many different kinds of ministry, and people have lifelong needs. Your training institution doesn't have the capacity or the calling to do everything for everybody. As we discussed in chapter 3, we need to know *our* mission and purpose. Careful thought and lots of prayer is needed before we move away from what we are good at to become something else. A Bible school with lots of students and a history of successful service to the church shouldn't transfer its energy and resources into becoming a graduate program for only a handful of potential students, especially if there are other options for advanced study within the region. Similarly, unless there are compelling reasons for change, a Bible school shouldn't neglect its own students as it shifts toward secular job training for the broader community. Our curricular plan will be the outworking of *our* values and purposes within *our* particular context.

2. Who Are We Trying to Equip?

We need to develop a profile of entering students to discover their calling, gifting, experience and previous training. To equip them well for ministry requires learning about them in three related areas – knowing, doing and being:

- What do they already know (and not just about the Bible and theology)?
- What do they already know how to do? What skills and abilities do they possess?
- What kind of people are they? What do we know about their maturity and character?

Having the answers to these three questions gives us a starting point from which to develop a curricular plan. However, before we start writing our curriculum, it is important to remember that we have control over who can enter our training programs. It is appropriate to ask students to meet certain requirements before we will admit them. If they don't have a certain level of educational training or a certain amount of experience in ministry, they may not have the learning tools and basic knowledge and skills to be able to learn along with other students. If a student is a new believer (or if it is questionable whether he or she is a believer at all), it doesn't make sense to begin training for positions of leadership in the church. Equally, if there is little sense of a calling to ministry or almost no experience in doing ministry in the church, it may be wise to not accept them (or least, not yet) as students. We don't have to start at whatever level the students bring us.

3. For What Are We Training?

Our purpose is to prepare our students for life and ministry. For us to develop a curricular plan for them, we need to understand what specific knowledge and competencies they will require to be effective in the ministry roles that they will assume. If they are becoming pastors, what are the many different things that pastors need to know how to do? If our students will become cross-cultural missionaries, what is it that they will need to know or know how to do in order to be effective? What attitudes and character are required in a cross-cultural missionary?

4. How Should We Get from Here to There?

This is the heart of what a curricular plan is: getting real students from where they are to where they need to be in order to minister effectively. Whether we offer them new information, train them in new skills or disciple them in right ways to live, everything that we include in our curriculum needs to contribute to getting our students from where they are to where they need to be. We do not simply teach courses because they have always been taught. Each course complements all other courses in order to equip our students for what it is that they will be doing.

During the late 1990s, three relatively small evangelical theological schools in Lebanon began discussing how they could share their faculty and facilities to better train their students. In order to do this, they needed a common curriculum for all three schools. Their first task was to determine a narrative profile of what they wanted their graduates to look like in areas of being, knowing and doing. They then analyzed every subject currently in their respective course catalogs to see how each of these contributed to producing the outcomes they wanted. Not all existing subjects fit, and so after two full years of discussion, the result was a new four-year BTh curriculum for all three schools.

The first year was a discipleship program focused on "being." The curriculum was designed to give an overview of the Bible, a firm understanding of one's faith and to instill regular habits of Bible study, prayer and evangelism in any Christian. Students were also introduced to lay ministry in the local church ("doing"), the focus on the second year of study. Second-year students learned basic skills in preaching, teaching, missions and administration and were introduced to church and denominational history. Both of these years concluded with a celebration of accomplishments and no hint of failure for those who did not go on to the next level. Only those who evidenced pastoral gifts and a call to ministry, and who successfully mastered the subjects of the first two years, were invited into the third and fourth years of the BTh curriculum. While the final two years had "knowing" as their major objective and were designed to provide foundations for those who would become leaders within the Middle Eastern context, each course still included being and doing components.

Three Basic Types of Curriculum

1. The Invisible Curriculum

The invisible, or hidden, curriculum is what we teach whether we intended to or not. One of the rules of education is that we tend to teach the way we were taught. In the same way, our students will imitate our attitudes, behaviors and teaching methodologies, even if we never said anything about them. They will learn about valuing time over people – or people over time – by the behavior of their teachers. They will learn about status by the size of our offices or by our titles or by the way we treat those "below" us. As we become aware of the things that we are really teaching, the curricular implication is that we should control what we can from our invisible curriculum so that we can intentionally guide our students into learning the right things.

2. The Null Curriculum

We don't teach everything that could be taught. The null curriculum is what we don't teach. Nevertheless, maybe some of those subjects that we don't offer could help to equip our students more adequately for ministry than some of the ones we have always taught. Our students and the environment in which they minister are constantly changing. Twenty-five years ago there wasn't a need to discuss ministry in a context of HIV-AIDS, though this is an urgent need now. What else should be included into our formal curriculum so that we don't fail to help our students learn about important issues that they will face in their ministries? The curricular implication is that when you add something, you need to drop something else that has now become less important.

3. The Visible Curriculum

The visible, or explicit, curriculum is the list of courses offered to students and listed in our prospectus. Most curricula in theological training institutions are built around five areas of study:

- Biblical studies (including languages)
- Theology
- Church history

- Practical studies, such as preaching, counseling, or church administration
- General studies, such as English, psychology or sociology

These are all things that are worth studying. However, the painful reality is that we have a limited amount of time in which to equip students for their ministries. Curriculum development can be a game of fill-in-the-blanks. For a three-year program, with four classes per term over six terms, there are twenty-four blanks to fill in with courses to be offered by teachers, with written syllabi, course objectives, a sequence of topics to be covered, assignments and assigned readings, etc. Most people tend to fill these slots with all the courses that *they* took when they were students, and they then teach them in the usual ways that these kinds of courses are always taught. This is not the best way to develop a curriculum. We need to make some difficult choices as we consciously think through what will get our students from where they are to where they need to be. Courses that offer foundational knowledge should be balanced with those that help to develop specific skills. All teachers need to know how each of their respective subjects fits together with everything else to equip students for ministry.

Our invisible curriculum (what students really learn, whether we intended to teach it or not) will contribute to this process as well. For example, as we train them for pastoral roles, what are we teaching about time management by the way we use time; about the importance of prayer in ministry by the way we pray; or about the importance of people by the relationships we maintain with others? Do we behave as shepherds or governors? Are we inadvertently teaching them to be humble pastors or to be arrogant bishops?

Character Development

Transforming the human heart is the work of God. So to what extent can a training program facilitate spiritual maturity in its students? Probably the most important answer arises from the extent to which we understand how our environment influences what we learn about everything. Our students (and faculty) will grow in Christ as they are part of a consciously Christian community where we take seriously God's presence among us.

A school's faculty and administrative teams should creatively work with each other to come up with ideas as to how spiritual growth and maturity can be encouraged among the students. Here are some suggestions that others have tried:

- Hire a dean of students who will serve as pastor and counselor to staff and students.
- Schedule regular spiritual activities, such as chapel or small prayer groups.
- Faculty can serve as one-on-one mentors of students, helping them develop plans for their own spiritual growth.
- Students can document their own spiritual growth through journaling.
- Develop and enforce rules for acceptable behavior for the academic community – and then discipline biblically those who violate the rules.
- Schedule special events, such as retreats, days of prayer or a week of special spiritual emphasis.
- Include classes in the curriculum relating to spiritual formation, such as on evangelism or the Christian family. A course on "prayer" could examine Scriptural teaching, or use books by those who prayed, or develop prayer exercises to help students evaluate their own prayer lives and develop new habits of prayer.
- Schedule a day each semester for teachers and staff to confidentially discuss issues related to the spiritual growth of each one of the students enrolled at the school. Then take time to pray for each student individually.
- Encourage and oversee integration between all subjects being taught. Teachers need to understand how their subject areas contribute to the overall curriculum, including the spiritual growth of students. How well does everything work together to effectively equip students in areas of character for the ministries that they will have?

Course Design

According to George Posner and Alan Rudnitsky, general educational goals explain why we are offering our program at all.[3] A curricular plan generically defines what we will be teaching, and is built around intended learning outcomes (ILOs). Our "why" should be visible in our institutional purpose while our "what" will be seen in the collection of courses that we include in our explicit curriculum. It is as we design an educational or instructional plan that we answer the question "how?"

To have overall excellence in our curriculum, each individual course within the curriculum must be well-designed and well-taught. There are many good resources that have been written to assist teachers in developing the courses they teach. I have listed some of these in the bibliography at the end of this chapter.

We don't automatically achieve excellence by importing curricular packages or programmed materials that others have designed. These may be brilliantly done and perhaps they can serve as resources for enriching our program. But if our concern is to equip *our* students for ministry, we need to be careful about simply adopting someone else's content and methodology without adapting these for the specific world and needs of our students.

As we will see in the next chapter, the greatest resource that any training program has is its teachers. Excellent training programs have great teachers who know how to use good materials to train their students. That is much more than being monitors who only make sure that students correctly fill in the blanks of their programmed teaching materials. Teachers build relationships with their students and apply truths to the lives of people that they have gotten to know. They need the freedom to draw on their own gifts and experiences as they develop courses that respond appropriately to the needs of their students.

The potential difficulty of allowing teachers as much freedom as they want is that each class subject must contribute to the agreed-upon process of the overall curriculum, that is, to get students from where they are to where they need to be. A program's curricular plan will define the content and the intended learning outcomes for the overall program. Each subject to be

---

3. George Posner and Alan Rudnitsky, *Course Design: A Guide to Curriculum Development for Teachers* (New York, NY: Longman, 2001).

taught should then have its own syllabus on file. This will have agreed-upon learning objectives, a narrative summary of what the subject is to cover and how the material fits into the overall curriculum of the training program. Whoever teaches the subject will develop his or her instructional plan on this standardized syllabus and then present this in written form to the students (and to files) as a plan for how the course will actually be taught.

For example, an individual assigned to teach the book of Romans may be given three intended learning objectives for the study of this biblical book: (a) that students will come to understand and affirm their own justification by faith; (b) that students will be able to explain a summary of the theology and thinking of Paul; and (c) that students will gain skills in inductive Bible study. A good teacher will fulfill the objectives for the course, while developing a creative class-time methodology, in accordance with his own skills. What he doesn't have is the freedom to only cover chapters 1–3, or to fail to adequately deal with all three of the objectives.

A Syllabus Needs to Include:

- Course description. This is the brief narrative description of what the course is to cover and the rationale as to how the course fits into the overall curriculum.
- Course objectives or goals. These are the agreed-upon intentional learning objectives for this subject matter.
- A schedule of what will be covered and when. This should include some indication of the methodologies that will be used in looking at various aspects of the subject matter. The schedule should also indicate dates for special events or exams, as well as due dates for assignments.
- The requirements for the course. What reading or projects will students need to do? Will there be case studies, group work or field trips? Will there be exams? The syllabus should indicate something of how these assignments will be evaluated and the weight that each assignment will have on the overall grade (along with things like attendance or class participation). Note that evaluations must be designed so that both the student and the teacher will know that the course objectives have been met.

- A list of the textbooks or required reading for the course, along with a bibliography of books, articles or electronic resources that could allow the student to explore the subject in greater detail.

A copy of the syllabus should be on file for every course included in the explicit curriculum of the theological training institution, that is, everything listed in the school's course catalog. It is also helpful to keep a confidential file in the office for academic administration that includes teaching notes, copies of exams and perhaps even examples of exceptionally good work done by students. Over time, this is the best way to document the quality of what is being done by teachers in implementing the curriculum. A complete file on each subject is also helpful for new teachers to be able to draw on the wisdom of those who have taught this before.

In the next chapter we will look at how to help teachers to teach better. We will then discuss further in chapter 12 how evaluation can be used to improve the curriculum.

Using Curricular Materials

It may be a lot of unnecessary work to write all of your own teaching materials when there is so much that has already been done by others. Nevertheless, as most authors were writing for an audience that is different than ours, we need to evaluate curricular materials before we use them. There are six key questions that a teacher should ask before deciding to use someone else's material:

1. What is the purpose of this material? Is there enough similarity so that it also can serve to meet my purposes in the course that I am teaching?
2. What assumptions have been made about the users? Are these assumptions that could describe my students, or are they too different for this textbook to be helpful to them?
3. What methodology is used, and is it appropriate for its intended users? Is it also appropriate for my students?
4. Is there a logical flow or sequence to what is presented? Is this sequence organized in a way that allows us to adequately cover what we need to do?

5. How could the materials best be used? Is our class structured in such a way that these materials will contribute to the learning of my students?
6. What hesitations do I have about the materials? Is there a bias? Are there limitations in what it will be able to do for my students?

Writing Your Own Curricular Materials

After a teacher has taught a particular subject for five years or so, he or she may feel ready to write up what has worked successfully in the classroom for others to benefit from the experience and wisdom. However, before you take on the difficult task of trying to write curricular materials, make sure that you are aware of what has already been done by others and why these existing materials aren't adequate. You need to be clear as to who needs your "curriculum" and why.

Curricular materials need to have a logical flow and sequencing and include suggestions for methodologies that are appropriate for those who will likely use the materials. Unlike what you presented as a teacher in class, written words will be read without the benefit of someone to explain what isn't clear. A manual or explanation of how to use your material may help, though even this will be read without your being present to explain it.

Find ways to get critical feedback from colleagues and friends concerning what you have written. It is best if you do the first test-teaching of your own materials, although before these materials are published, they should also be test-taught by others who can provide feedback about what was confusing or difficult to use.

Conclusions

Your students come from and go into an environment that is constantly changing. Thus the profile of your students will change over time, as will the profile of what your graduates will need to know, and know what to do and be. These changes require you to regularly rethink (and not just perfect) your curriculum, in order to help your students get from where they are now to where they will need to be in three to five years. Thus, it is good to revise (or at least revisit) the entire curriculum every five years or so.

Becoming an excellent theological education institution requires courage and creativity. Your curriculum should not primarily reflect the traditions from your glorious past, but should be an integrated and deliberate way to equip the real people who are studying now for the real ministries that they will have. Your graduates will rise up and call you blessed!

Discussion Questions Regarding Your Curriculum

1. As you reflect on the impact of your training program, what has been your particular role within the curricular plan that God has for your students?
2. If you have never done this before (or if you haven't done this recently), develop a composite profile of the students who come to study with you. What do they know? What do they know how to do? What kinds of people are they?
3. Do you have students who probably shouldn't have been admitted because they don't fit this profile?
4. What do your graduates do when they finish their training with you? If you have never done this before (or if you haven't done this recently), develop a composite profile of what a graduate needs to know, know how to do or be for effectiveness in the ministries that God has for them.
5. To what extent is your curricular plan helping to get your students from here to there so that they are adequately equipped for real ministry? Or to what extent is the problem "with the curriculum" as was stated at the beginning of this chapter?

Suggestions for Further Reading

Alstete, Jeffrey W. *Accreditation Matters: Achieving Academic Recognition and Renewal.* Jossey-Bass: ASHE-ERIC Higher Education Report, Vol. 30, no. 4 (2004).

Bates, A. W., and Gary Poole. *Effective Teaching with Technology in Higher Education.* San Francisco, CA: Jossey-Bass, 2003.

Cole, Victor B. *Training of the Ministry.* Bangalore: Theological Book Trust, 2001.

Downs, P. G. *Teaching for Spiritual Growth: An Introduction to Christian Education.* Grand Rapids, MI: Zondervan, 1994.

Fisher, L. A., and C. Levene. *Planning a Professional Curriculum.* Calgary, Alberta: University of Calgary Press, 1989.

Ford, L. A. *Curriculum Design Manual for Theological Education: A Learning Outcomes Focus.* Nashville, TN: Broadman, 1991.

Gangel, Kenneth, and James Wilhoit. *The Christian Educator's Handbook on Adult Education.* Wheaton, IL: Victor Press, 1993.

Habermas, R., and K. Issler. *Teaching for Reconciliation: Foundations and Practice of Christian Educational Ministry.* Grand Rapids, MI: Baker, 1992.

Harris, M. *Fashion Me a People: Curriculum in the Church.* Louisville, KY: Westminster, 1989.

Hart, D. G., and R. Albert Mohler, Jr. *Theological Education in the Evangelical Tradition.* Grand Rapids, MI: Baker, 1996.

Langford, David P., and Barbara A. Cleary. *Orchestrating Learning with Quality.* Milwaukee, WI: ASQC Quality Press, 1995.

Lewy, Arieh. *Handbook of Curriculum Evaluation.* New York, NY: UNESCO and the International Institute of Educational Planning, 1977.

Leypoldt, Martha M. *Learning Is Change: Adult Education in the Church.* Valley Forge, PA: Judson Press, 1971.

Posner, George J., and Alan H. Rudnitsky. *Course Design: A Guide to Curriculum Development for Teachers.* New York, NY: Longman, 2001.

Theological and Christian Education Commission (TCEC). Training God's Servants: A Compendium of the Papers and Findings of a Workshop on "Training for Missions in Africa." Nairobi: Association of Evangelicals in Africa, 1997.

Toohey, S. *Designing Courses for Higher Education.* Buckingham, UK: Open University Press, 1999.

Vella, Jane. *How Do They Know That They Know.* San Francisco, CA: Jossey-Bass, 1998.

———. *Learning to Listen, Learning to Teach.* San Francisco, CA: Jossey-Bass, 1994.

Wiggins, Grant and Jay McTighe. *Understanding by Design.* Alexandria, VA: Association for Supervision and Curriculum Development, 1998.

7

Excellence in Teachers

The most important single resource that a program has is its teaching team. Excellent training institutions know how to find, train and encourage their teachers.

According to Ephesians 4:11, teachers are a gift from God to the church to help his people learn to put truth into the practice of their daily lives. If it is true that the focus of our educational efforts should be on character development and ministry preparation, then we need teachers who know how to do this well. We don't need teachers who simply read students the notes from their own seminary classes. How can we discover the kinds of educators that we need? The best place to start may be with the teaching staff that we already have, although in many training programs this can be a rather motley collection of "free" missionaries along with a handful of full- and part-time local teachers. Helping this group become more effective in what they are trying to do cannot be accomplished solely by sending them all off for advanced graduate degrees.

I prefer the term *teacher* to that of *professor*, *lecturer* or *tutor*. There is some appeal in having the specialized, individualized attention of a tutor, though for many people the term primarily connotes those who listen passively as undergraduates recite their lessons. A "professor" tends to be a term of status given to someone with lots of formal education after long years of tenure. It may or may not indicate what the person can actually do. The term "lecturer," however, describes exactly what the person does: lecture. We don't need someone to read to our students what they should be able to read on their own at home or in the library. On the other hand, the term "teacher" theoretically describes someone who helps students to learn.

Good teachers are the greatest resource that any school or training program has. We are blessed if we have teachers who know how to pastorally care for and equip students so that they will be ready to take on the ministries to which God has called them. We need those who know their subject matter well and who model what they know. We also want them to know the techniques of teaching so that they can creatively help their students explore the real world, as well as the world of ideas and books. Excellent training programs know how to develop their teaching staff into these kinds of people.

Factors in Developing the Faculty That We Need

An institution may have an adequate number of people for the courses it offers without having a really good faculty team. All of our teachers may have advanced degrees. We even have the right percentage of national staff, yet our faculty may remain inadequate. Five questions help us determine whether our teachers contribute to our having an excellent faculty team.

1. Do They Have Formal Training in the Right Areas?

Obtaining advanced-level degrees is important, although the relevance of one's advanced training is even more important. Does what was studied have anything to do with the area in which the person will actually be teaching? We need teachers who have a depth of knowledge about *their* area of instruction, not simply those who have demonstrated a capacity to make it through academic hoops. Having a PhD in mathematics or medicine does not qualify someone to teach biblical studies or church history.

Nevertheless, there is much value when teachers have learned how to think and do research in their areas of teaching under the guidance of a competent mentor and when their degrees come from credible institutions. Advanced study helps people to acquire a broad understanding of issues that will be relevant to students, while the models of learning that they observe while they study enhances their own program when they teach.

2. Do They Have Practical Skills in the Right Areas?

What does a teacher actually know how to do in the area where he or she will be teaching? It is reasonable to expect that a homiletics teacher actually knows how to preach, that pastoral pragmatics are being taught by pastors, that counseling courses are being offered by those with training and experience in listening, that evangelism is being taught by those who regularly share their faith, and that missiology is being taught by those who have experience in cross-cultural ministry.

Communications is also a skill that should be required in our teachers. We aren't helped by having people on staff with advanced degrees and lots of knowledge if what they know can't be communicated coherently at the level of the students. This includes linguistic competency. I have met missionary teachers who were brilliant in what they knew, but who so rarely spoke the language of instruction outside of class that they could hardly speak it in class. This is unfair to students. Some exceptions can be made for visiting professors who are experts in a specific area, but a faculty is not adequate if it is primarily made up of those who cannot communicate what they know to students in any language.

3. Are They Good Role Models?

The catalog or prospectus of every seminary or Bible school describes the spiritual growth that they hope to see in their students during their time of study. The single greatest factor that contributes to spiritual growth seems to be what students see in the lives and ministries of their teachers. How well does your faculty do in what they are modeling?

Timothy was to be an example in speech, life, love, faith and purity. His growth was to be so public that everyone and anyone could monitor his progress (1 Tim 4:12–16). To what extent are our faculty members committed to knowing and loving God? Are students able to see their teachers grow spiritually? Or to what extent are our teachers like the elders Paul described in 1 Timothy 3 – above reproach and respected by all? What do their families and marriages look like? Do our teachers regularly participate in local churches? Do they respect each other, or do they say negative things about one another both in and out of class? Do they respect their students, or do they only show up for class, being "too busy" for their students at any other time?

These things matter, as who we are speaks much louder than anything we verbalize. When Jesus warned of false teachers in Matthew 7, nothing was said about the content of the lectures that they gave. Scripture speaks in other places about the importance of truth and correct doctrine. Yet, a false teacher is also known by the fruit that everyone can see in his or her life. We will learn about the excellence of our teaching staff as we ourselves observe them, and as we listen to appropriate evaluations about them from students and colleagues.

4. Are They Gifted for Teaching?

We have already noted that teachers are special people, given by God to prepare his people for ministry (Eph 4:11-16). These teachers who are pastors – or pastors who are teachers – draw on their experiences and the Scriptures to help their students become mature, equipped for every good work (2 Tim 3:17).

Are those whom you have contracted to teach actually gifted by God for teaching? Although we can distinguish the gifting of a person as a teacher from skills that can be learned in order to teach more effectively, the two are related. All of us (including those gifted by God to be teachers) can learn more about the basic rules of pedagogy in order to more creatively facilitate the learning process of others. Nevertheless, it would seem reasonable that training programs should have faculty who are those pastor/teachers that God has given to his church as a gift. We should be able to discern who these people are through the evidence that they are being used by God to equip others for ministry.

5. Are They Willing to Grow?

Every teacher should have a curiosity to know more, a longing to mature in obedience, and a desire to improve his or her teaching methodology. One big hindrance to this comes from pride, the feeling that we already know enough. I knew a medical doctor in Latin America who had not read anything new about medicine since completing his studies years earlier. He's not unique, but can anyone seriously want to be treated by such a person?

Are our teachers so very different? Some instructors are afraid of discussion lest a student ask something they don't already know. Classes routinely can be taught by someone who hasn't changed a thing since he or she began teaching 35 years ago. An adequate teaching faculty is composed of those who constantly learn new things by listening and observing, with an internal commitment to keep on growing and to do things even better. As a new missionary, I visited a colleague who had been in Brazil for a number of years and who had taught in several different locations. I asked if I could sit in on his classes to learn more about how to teach in the Brazilian context. As we talked afterwards, he commented with tears in his eyes, "You know, you are the first person who has ever observed one of my classes."

All elementary and secondary level teachers undergo rigorous on-site practical training to prepare them for their teaching responsibilities. Most also need to participate in regular re-training once they begin to teach. This rarely happens for those who work in Bible schools or for those who teach in universities. Somehow a PhD, all by itself, theoretically qualifies a person to be a tertiary level lecturer almost anywhere, even though many with PhDs don't have a clue about how to teach effectively. Becoming and staying excellent requires that our qualified teaching staff be committed to continue to grow.

A really good teaching team is the product of a well-constructed strategic plan. As we learn about who our new students are, discovering what they know and know how to do, and as we discern who they will need to be when they graduate with specific knowledge and skills – getting them from here to there requires the right kind of teachers and mentors.

We should begin our assessment of the excellence of our teachers by looking closely at the teachers we already have. For most, we will be able to affirm with joy how God is using them as we look for ways that we can help them become even more effective. However, not everyone with a degree is worth having as a teacher. If we conclude that some of those on our teaching team are not the right people to help us get our students from where they are to where they need to be, we need the courage and tact to weed them out. Letting people go is not easy in any culture. It may not even be legal to release a staff member. Nevertheless, through prayer and wisdom, it is possible to find ways to encourage those who don't fit in to leave. There's too much at stake if you don't have the right kind of team.

Caring for the Teachers That We Have

If teachers are satisfied and content, they will not move away from us so quickly to new pastures. Satisfaction is more likely to occur when they are a part of a healthy living and working environment. So how can a training institution be the kind of place where excellent teachers want to work and in which they can continue to grow and develop? There are seven areas that will help our teachers to feel comfortable and satisfied that they are part of an excellent teaching team.

1. Are We Clear about Our Identity, Purpose and Expectations?

Excellent training programs know why they exist. Their programs are coherently constructed to respond to the real needs of the community they are serving. Their curriculum is designed and regularly updated to help students to get from where they are to where they need to go. New people are oriented to the program's history, ethos and practices. Job descriptions exist and each person knows what they do and how this contributes to the overall purpose of the training program. Participation together in a task that we know is worth doing is a great way to make a training program attractive to those teachers that we want to come and stay.

2. Do We Provide Adequately for the Necessities of Life?

We will discuss this further in chapter 10, but issues of salary and housing are important in finding and keeping the kind of faculty that we want. We need to consider the education of their children as well as health care and retirement funding. If we have been considerate and wise in developing appropriate support packages for our staff, we will be attractive to them and successful in finding and keeping the right kind of staff.

3. Do We Function Well as a Caring Community?

Who we are as a community not only speaks loudly to our students, it also is important to our teachers and staff. To retain and encourage excellent teaching teams, we need to be healthy communities that know how to encourage and minister to one another. Open communication needs to be modeled throughout the academic community. Conflicts need to be resolved through individual efforts, with gentle intervention if necessary. Both students and staff should receive pastoral care, with structured time for prayer and sharing. Time needs to be built into job descriptions to allow for activities that will develop and strengthen community. Our communities should be enjoyable places to live and work.

4. Are We a Learning Community?

We will discuss excellence in renewal in chapter 12, but it is worth remembering that good teachers are those who continue to learn. Excellent programs schedule and encourage participation in a variety of on- and off-campus activities to help teachers stay sharp and to teach better. You may want to host seminars with outside specialists, have guided discussions around key issues, or share the research that various staff members are working on. Time should be allocated for research and writing if this is expected as a part of the teaching task. Formal study can be a part of ongoing learning as well as a chance for renewal as it allows a person to take something in, rather than constantly give out. We will discuss formal advanced training later in this chapter.

5. Do We Encourage Breaks and Taking Time for Renewal?

Being a good teacher requires a lot of work. There are two issues here. The first is that a teacher must be given time in order to stay on top of what will best equip each new generation of students for the ministries that they will have. We don't want our teachers doing the same things in the same ways year after year. Teachers and staff need time for reflection, as well as for research and reading in order to better understand and communicate what they are teaching.

But the many activities of being a teacher can also be draining. An accumulation of spiritual and emotional exhaustion results in ineffective and unhappy people. Some may opt to leave the education world entirely, at least for a while. People should not be encouraged to work twenty-four hours a day, every day of the week. We need to encourage days off and the regular taking of vacation days. Time for longer breaks will also help. Missionaries are usually allowed regular long-leave, although not all missionaries use this time wisely for renewal and rest. However, little is ever arranged for national staff. Structuring and funding periodic breaks for both refreshment and renewal, often called sabbaticals, would help us to hold onto a staff that will be healthier and more productive.

6. Do We Encourage Networking?

Participation in regional training conferences and consultations are excellent ways for people to learn new ideas and skills. Morale and the quality of teaching is improved when staff can build relationships with colleagues at other training programs in the region. Participation in consultations also honors your staff as they gain status and recognition as they make presentations concerning what they (and you) have learned and done. Allowing our teaching team to occasionally offer their courses in other training institutions also honors them, while encouraging renewal through a periodic change of scenery. Furthermore, faculty exchanges make economic sense as we share our expertise while borrowing the expertise of others. Such networking is a good way to learn new insights as we see how others do what we are also trying to do.

Making all this happen requires giving faculty time, as well as occasionally helping with funding. This kind of investment will help you keep your best teachers.

7. Do We Have Good Library Resources?

Those who return from study overseas often complain that they no longer have access to the wonderful resources they had there. We don't need to duplicate overseas libraries, but providing reference books and appropriate journals, along with a capacity for electronic research will allow our faculty to continue to study and grow. We will discuss excellence in libraries in chapter 9.

Finding New Teachers

Assuming that you have determined what kind of people you want and that you have a clear sense of what you want them to do, there are several different ways to find the right kinds of teachers for your training program.

1. Grow Your Own Teachers

One of Africa's better master's level training programs intentionally watches its students to see if any of them have the gifts and abilities to become a teacher. As they approach graduation the school invites one or two of these to stay on for an additional year as teaching assistants. During that year they do some supervised teaching, as well as being exposed to the activities and responsibilities involved in being a faculty member. If a person shows interest and exceptional aptitude, the school looks for scholarship money for further formal training. Upon finishing these studies, the former student returns to become a full-time faculty member. They fit in well precisely because they know the school and its needs. This system has worked well, and so far there hasn't been any brain drain along the way. Even for those teaching assistants who aren't invited to stay on, they have learned valuable things about what it means to be a faculty member.

2. Use Modular Teachers

Not every institution needs its own specialists for every area of study. Exchanging faculty who can teach intensive modular courses in each other's schools is one way to share the wealth of those who are qualified in specific areas. We can also tap into regional or international specialists who are willing to teach modular courses, especially if we provide (or at least offer) funding for travel, hospitality and a reasonable honorarium. Through the push for internationalization, some overseas training institutions have encouraged their faculty to get international experience. Funding to cover most of their costs may be available through the visiting professor's institution or through his or her home church.

However, remember that not every free or available teacher is an expert, and that even "experts" can vary tremendously in their ability to teach, especially in cross-cultural environments. Neither is a training program enhanced when too much of its teaching is done via translation. If you aren't satisfied with what is being done, don't forget that you have the option to not invite them to teach again.

3. Take Advantage of Local Practitioners

For most teachers in the non-Western world, teaching is only one of the many things that they do. Much of our teaching staff may be made up of part-time local people. This can be very beneficial to the program as these individuals are normally immersed in full-time ministries, further exposing our students to the day-to-day realities of doing ministry. We need to discover who it is that has expertise that can be borrowed so as to enrich our training program. There can also be financial advantages in borrowing teachers from other organizations, churches and missions, as we don't need to provide for their housing or for the broader social packages required for full-time employees.

However, even good teachers may not find enough time to prepare for their classes if their primary occupation keeps them too busy elsewhere. I have heard students complain about big-name denominational or organizational leaders who either don't show up for their class or come poorly prepared. It is also difficult for both part-time teachers and visiting faculty to become a part of the school's community or to develop deep mentoring relationships with students.

4. Recruit and Hire the Best Teachers You Can Find

At least in Africa, but perhaps everywhere in the non-Western world, church and school leadership are quite aware of who has teaching gifts. We may discover that some of our most gifted part-time teachers, or those who teach wonderfully in occasional modular courses, are interested in teaching full-time. Our problem is often not a lack of qualified people who are available, but a way to actually hire them. As we will discuss in chapter 10, we need to strengthen our finances and our facilities, so that we can acquire and hold onto an adequate faculty. It is better when a school can hire (and fire) its own teachers rather than be dependent on staff who have raised their own support. People tend to work for those who pay them, and if we are not the ones paying them, they don't really work for us. It is awkward to develop and manage a teaching team made up of "free" people who have been offered to us. At the minimum, "free" teachers (including missionaries) should have a signed contract with the training program that indicates their agreement (and that of their sponsoring agencies) to fulfill all the obligations of the job description.

One way to avoid hiring bad teachers is to observe them professionally and personally before bringing them into a permanent position. We obviously must examine qualifications and hear recommendations about someone before considering adding that person to our teaching team. But it is also good to watch and to get to know someone before hiring him or her. A potential faculty member can be invited to give a series of special lectures or to offer an intensive modular course. Students and colleagues can provide commentary on issues of character, relationships, communication, pedagogy or knowledge of the subject matter. A potential faculty member can also be included in a variety of campus and social activities to see how well the person fits into the community and its ethos.

This applies to missionaries as well. Even if the teaching has to be done through a translator, if at all possible, the potential missionary teacher should be required to visit in this way. Even when a visit is not possible, all new faculty members, including missionaries, should be given a period of probation so that their life and practice can be seen. It is much easier to never hire the wrong person than to try to get rid of someone who shouldn't be there.

5. Develop Mission Partnerships

Most non-Western training programs have close ties with mission organizations and with their respective church denominations. Our training programs may provide much of the upper-level leadership for these organizations and churches, yet few of them provide teachers in return. We need to challenge them to either provide funds so that we can hire some of the quality people who are available or to nominate or loan a quality person that we can consider in the same way that we consider any other potential faculty member.

Formal Faculty Development – Advanced Study

Everyone is aware of the financial costs of studying overseas, of the dangers of non-contextualized training and of brain drain. It is encouraging that many of the better students seem to be opting to study in quality upper-level training programs that are a lot closer to home. So what should be the role of a training institution in encouraging the formal development of its own faculty? The following questions are important in considering issues of advanced study for teachers.

1. Who Decides Whether a Particular Person Should Pursue Advanced Study?

In North America, Western Europe and much of Latin America, a student simply applies to wherever he or she wants to study. At the other extreme, our church in Mozambique selected all of our students for us. No one else (neither the school nor the students) had a say in who our students were to be. We thus ended up with relatives of pastors, some of whom had little desire to even be there. Neither of these extremes is ideal.

The seminary or Bible school community where the individual is already a teacher should take responsibility for encouraging the development of its faculty team. We need a general master plan that prioritizes the continuing education of all of our staff. An individual may express his or her desire to receive further training, but it is our responsibility as an institution to evaluate that request in the light of our faculty needs and in the light of our perception of the individual's capacity as a teacher. Although people are free to negotiate their own further study wherever they want, it is the training institution that should manage the master plan as to who does advanced study with the blessing and financial encouragement of the institution. It is also an invitation to misunderstanding and brain drain if we allow donors or organizations to pick their own candidates to study in contexts that may be far away from the home culture.

2. What Options Exist Other Than Long-Term Training Programs in The West?

If a piece of paper is all that your faculty needs, perhaps the easiest option is to purchase a doctoral degree (with minimal or no work required) for $100 or so in cash from any number of questionable programs in certain parts of the non-Western world. However, if it is also important to learn something, be encouraged that quality upper-level programs can increasingly be found at locations around the world. It is also possible to do in-context extension training with many international training programs. Do your homework carefully before opting to send someone away for advanced-level study. There is no case where I would recommend sending someone overseas for study at the bachelor's or even master's level, despite the enticement of generous scholarships from overseas programs. Although their desire is to have a culturally rich and enjoyable learning environment for their students, the reality is that few foreign students receive the kind of attention that will practically equip them for the ministries that they will have back home.

There is more justification for overseas study at upper levels, such as for a ThM or PhD, or in specialized areas of interest. It can be helpful to broaden horizons, to develop lifelong relationships with international colleagues, to work under internationally-recognized mentors, or to have easy access to research. All of these may outweigh the disadvantages of context and cost. Some even find that study in the West is a good opportunity to develop relationships with potential long-term donors for their projects back home. You may conclude that these reasons are compelling enough to send your faculty far away for study. However, as many first-rate scholars and mentors have returned home to work and as the nature of how research can be done is rapidly changing through the Internet (and inexpensive flights), there are lots of options that offer first-rate training within the context. These options include a growing number of evangelical doctoral programs regionally as well as options through quality secular local universities. Don't rush off for that which may not be the best, before carefully looking at what else is available!

3. If They Do Go, How Can Contextual Dislocation Be Minimized?

Being a foreign student is often difficult and lonely. One of the most important ways to help those who have gone overseas for study is to maintain regular contact with them. This includes remembering them with regular email, and holding special times of prayer for their needs. As leaders travel in their area, they should go out of their way to visit them. If it is possible to build travel into their scholarships, they should periodically come home in order to stay in touch with the reality in which they will teach, as well as to allow others to maintain a high level of confidence in them.

Better training programs have someone to serve as counselor or advisor to foreign students. All academic mentors need to be trained to know how to help their advisees apply their research and learning to their own specific needs. Each of those who have been selected to be Langham scholars are blessed to have prayer and support teams in the locations where they are studying. Team members regularly invite students into their homes and churches and check to see if they need help with the details of life in a foreign place. Langham also finds ways to encourage interaction between foreign students, including provoking discussion to help them reflect on how what they are learning fits in with the needs and realities of where they come from.

4. How Can Advanced Faculty Training Be Funded?

He who pays the piper decides what tune will be played. It is important to know who is paying for the scholarship and how, as this may influence who the faculty member views as his real employer upon graduation. Since it is difficult for donors to not have an agenda, do your best to use their agendas for the good of your Bible school. Faculty development should be part of your strategic and financial plan. It is appropriate for you to continue to provide housing and salary for the family of the person doing advanced-level study. It is the training program (and not primarily the individual) who should approach friends, churches, foundations and the advanced training program itself for assistance in training its faculty members. Scholarship funds should be managed by the school, not by the individual faculty member. This doesn't suggest that those who go to study (or their churches or families) should not be a part of the fundraising efforts. We place value on that which costs us something. However, it may be best to encourage them to raise funds for things like books that they will want to buy for themselves or for their personal living expenses, leaving the responsibility of funds for study and travel with the faculty member's training institution.

You will affirm your teachers as you invest in them through helping them to do further study. They will return to you with gratitude if you do an adequate job of helping to see that their needs are met during their time of formal study.

One Advantage of Investing in Your Teachers

The Institut Supérieur Théologique de Bunia (ISTB), located in the northeastern part of the Democratic Republic of the Congo, is a training institution caught in the middle of political and economic chaos during the last decade. Since 1961, ISTB has been a quality program serving a number of evangelical denominations, offering an undergraduate degree in theology and a two-year master's program. The school managed to stay open, even when the war entered the city of Bunia itself.

The political instability of the country made it almost impossible for foreign missionaries or visitors to teach at the school. Accordingly, ISTB made a strategic commitment to develop its own teachers, as these won't have to go away should the situation again become difficult. Between 1996 and 2005, they sent at least eight of their faculty members for further study. At the doctoral level, three were sent for study in South Africa, one to France and one to the US. At the master's level, three were sent to Kenya while one student went to a sister seminary in the Central African Republic. As of this writing, all have returned home to teach.

Conclusions

It is imperative that excellent theological training programs have an adequate faculty, teachers who are committed to continue learning and growing throughout their careers. Formal advanced-level faculty training is only one part of this process. A training institution needs to develop and nurture an environment where teachers can work comfortably and effectively. It needs to be courageous to weed out those who don't fit in and careful in finding and developing those who do. It also needs to be proactive in structuring and funding ongoing training opportunities, both formally and informally, for its entire faculty. Developing and maintaining an excellent faculty team is probably the most important thing that you can do to strengthen your training program and institution.

Discussion Questions Regarding Your Teachers

1. Are your faculty "teachers," "professors" or "lecturers"? Why do you say this?
2. To what extent do you have an adequate faculty? What are the biggest obstacles that keep you from having a more adequate teaching team? What could be done to strengthen the faculty that you have?
3. How well do you care for your teachers so that they joyfully want to serve as a part of your learning community?

4. What could be done to help your teachers do a better job of growing, as well as to be emotionally and spiritually healthy?
5. Do you have a plan for advanced faculty training? How well does it work?

Suggestions for Further Reading

Boice, Robert. *The New Faculty Member: Supporting and Fostering Faculty Development*. San Francisco, CA: Jossey-Bass, 1992.

Bright, David F., and Mary P. Richards. "Faculty Development." In *The Academic Deanship*, edited by David F. Bright and Mary P. Richards, 148–177. San Francisco, CA: Jossey-Bass, 2001.

Collins, Jim. *Good to Great*. New York, NY: Harper Collins, 2001.

Gangel, Kenneth O., and Howard G. Hendricks. *The Christian Educators Handbook on Teaching*. Grand Rapids, MI: Baker, 1988.

Hendricks, Howard G. *The 7 Laws of the Teacher*. Atlanta, GA: Walk Thru the Bible Ministries, 1987.

Lucas, Ann F., and Associates. *Leading Academic Change: Essential Roles for Department Chairs*. San Francisco: Jossey-Bass, 2000.

Maslach, Christina, and Michael P. Leiter. *The Truth about Burnout*. San Francisco, CA: Jossey-Bass, 1997.

Middaugh, Michael F. *Understanding Faculty Productivity: Standards and Benchmarks for Colleges and Universities*. San Francisco, CA: Jossey-Bass, 2001.

Wilkinson, Bruce H. *The 7 Laws of the Learner*. Portland, OR: Multnomah Press, 1992.

8

Excellence in Facilities

Excellent training institutions have adequate academic, administrative and research facilities that are maintained properly.

Not every training program needs a campus. But it does need to exist somewhere. Even if most classes are offered at off-site training locations using educational technology or part-time teachers, the school still has to have a base. While many creative training programs began in borrowed facilities, sooner or later they need a place they can call "home." The bare minimum requires office space for the administrative staff, files and records, along with an adequate library to serve the educational programs being offered. They probably also need at least one reasonably sized seminar room for thinking together, for staff and teacher training, or perhaps for an occasional modular class. These basics could easily be expanded to include housing for staff or for visiting teachers. But if you are not a residential campus, don't become a residential compound!

Bigger is not better. As we will note in chapter 11, the changing nature of adult education, coupled with the tools of educational technology mean that training increasingly happens at multiple locations. Training programs of the future are likely to function as theological resource centers serving a number of off-site programs, rather than as a single location where all teachers, classes, books and students can be found. We may discover that we will need less space in the future than we do now, though with some significant reorganizing of the space we have.

It should not be a requirement for a principal to possess all the skills of a building contractor. However, as facilities tend to be among the largest projects and expenditures that training programs have, the leadership of these programs needs to understand the issues involved in having and maintaining excellent facilities. In this chapter we want to think about how well we use and care for what we have. As we noted in chapter 3, a site plan is part of a strategic plan. But what image do we project through our facilities? How can we develop, administer and fund the right kinds of projects in order to have what we need?

Using Your Space Effectively

The strategic plan for your training institution should identify how much space, and what kind of space, you need in order to do what you intend to do. If money were no issue at all, it would be tempting for most schools to simply start over in a new location. Most of our campuses, large and small, were not designed by anyone. They are simply a random collection of buildings built at different periods of time during the school's history with whatever funds were available at the time. However, before you decide to start over, it is worth analyzing the adequacy of what you have. To what extent are you using your space well? Bear in mind that it can be helpful to have an office administrator who can sort out who it is that gets which office, etc. Nevertheless, could what you already have serve better if it were to be remodeled or reconfigured?

Your strategic plan should also estimate how much space, and what kind of space, you will need to have in five to ten years. Your implementation plan should include specific suggestions as to what should be modified and what needs to be built. This plan will not only estimate costs involved, but will make suggestions as to who should have responsibility for this and how funding can be found. Blessed is the training program that has put together a good strategic plan!

Site Plans

A site plan maps out the details of what your overall campus should look like in the future. It is good when students, faculty and staff dream about the future of their campus, though a site plan usually needs the input of an expert. Perhaps there are local or overseas friends with competence who will volunteer to help you do this, but this is important enough that it may be worth hiring someone with the requisite knowledge and skills to do it right. How much capacity will be needed for electricity, telephone, water or sewage, and where should these be placed (or not placed)? Does the ground in all areas allow for proper foundations for buildings? What kinds of walkways or roads will be needed for the normal flow of students and others? Are there legal requirements regarding roads or parking? Is there a maximum size for buildings that can be placed on a particular piece of property? Are there zoning issues that allow for some kinds of buildings, but not for others? What is more or less affordable in the appearance that might be desired in public buildings such as the chapel or auditorium? How close should student or faculty housing be to each other and to all other buildings? Will there be noise that will distract students from studying, or unhealthy pollution from factories? Etc. Most of us wouldn't have a clue as to how to answer these questions. We need the expert advice of those who can help us find the answers to questions like these. It is foolish to begin a project if you don't have a long-term site plan and a clear sense as to what can and cannot be done.

Maintenance Plans and Budgets

A friend of mine stayed in a guesthouse at a Bible school that actually began to fall apart during the night that he was there. (I have seen the pictures of the caved-in wall and fallen roof!) That's not excellence in facilities. We should not manage our resources by crisis, scrambling desperately to do maintenance that should have been taken care of yesterday. It is imperative to have a staff person with practical and organizational skills who can oversee our facilities and properties. There also should be a plan with a budget to make sure that what we have is appropriately cared for. Training programs may raise massive funding for the construction of a new building, while not having any idea as to how their new building will be maintained once it is built. Sadly, it is often easier to raise funds for building something new than to find donor sources for maintaining buildings. I know of at least two campuses that were built in accordance with the dreams of donors. The school neither needed that much space, nor can it now afford to maintain what it has. We should not build what we cannot take care of.

What Image Are You Trying to Give?

It is possible to build faculty offices, chapels or a library that are inappropriate to our purpose. A church leader once expressed shock to me at the student housing we had at one of our Bible schools. The rooms were not ostentatious, but his feeling was that we were creating expectations that would contribute to the graduates no longer being willing to serve in the denomination's churches, unless they could have housing like this (or better). This doesn't suggest that we sacrifice security or beauty in order to do things as cheaply as possible. Yet it is easy to overbuild. Bible schools shouldn't become monuments to themselves or to those donors who love to invest in massive projects that they can put their own names on.

It is important to balance campus development with program development. Large or expensive-looking offices, chapels or libraries may discourage churches and smaller donors from helping with operational costs as they sense that the school already has enough funding as seen in the beautiful buildings and offices that they have. Inappropriate facilities may also contribute to internal resentment, as staff or students feel that the school's leadership is more interested in finding money for construction than for salaries or for student textbooks. Certain types of buildings may even be subject to taxes that schools shouldn't normally need to pay.

Appropriate Building Projects

Projects need to make sense in function and size, given the number of students, faculty or staff that will be served. It is cheaper to fly every single one of your doctoral students to an overseas library once a year than to invest huge funds in research materials that might be used by only one graduate student every ten years or so. You don't need dormitories or classrooms that will accommodate 500 if you currently only have an enrollment of 50.

It is also important to make sure that the project is appropriate for your cultural context as well as being a reflection of your goals and values. A training program in Kenya was being pushed by authorities to build different sized offices for each of the many different categories of workers that the school had. In accordance with cultural norms that showed greater honor to people of greater importance, the school was told that the principal's office was to be slightly larger than the vice-principal's, which was to be larger than faculty offices, which were to be larger than secretarial offices, etc. Besides being a costly way to build an administrative building, this undermined the school's commitment to equality among its staff. The school stuck to its values, and was able to argue successfully for something much simpler.

Appropriate construction should obviously bear in mind local climatic conditions. Outside "experts" may not know how to build without including unnecessary and expensive centralized heating or air conditioning. In areas of intense heat, buildings probably have open courtyards, with high ceilings and carefully placed windows for natural ventilation. Local contractors will understand how to design structures to avoid the heat of direct sunlight in the summer while taking advantage of it in the winter. They will also understand things like prevailing winds and how to avoid both the noise and penetration of heavy rains.

Well-designed Building Projects

Before a building project can be initiated, our ideas and sketches need to become blueprints and master plans that will need to pass through multiple layers of officialdom. You will need expert help to do this correctly, perhaps even your own on-site building manager to be your advocate through the process. Government regulations and permits need to be obtained. Verification will be needed to show that no unusual site conditions exist or that there are no potential complications with roads, landscaping, drainage or access to utilities, such as electricity water and sewer. Buildings may need special certification to be wired for Internet or internal communications. Security issues can be very complicated as they affect different aspects of a project. Sorting through legal contracts may require the help of a lawyer.

Multiple bids will be needed to find a competent and sympathetic building contractor (who most likely should not be a close relative of one of your school's leaders). You may discover that hiring local contractors and using local workers is not only cheaper, but it can be a good way to develop positive feelings towards you and your program from the community.

Along with a plan for ongoing maintenance, good project design also requires thinking through what furnishings a new facility will need – tables and chairs, white boards, computers, etc. There's not much point in having a fancy new building if it can't be used!

Funding Your Building Projects

Construction projects normally require major fundraising efforts. The key to being effective is in demonstrating how your program will be a better program because of this particular project. This is another way of stating that all building projects need to grow directly out of your strategic plan.

It is not wise to start building until you have adequate funding, or secure promises of funding, in hand. It can be a bit of a dance to achieve this as one can't develop specific plans without clear promises of funding, and most donors won't make promises until they know that there are specific plans. One also needs funds to raise funds, as donors often won't promise their part until they know of the promises or gifts that others have already made.

We will discuss fundraising more in chapter 10. However, note that it is good to begin any fundraising project by visibly involving lots of local people. On the basis of local giving and local enthusiasm, there is a higher probability that international donors will also become interested in your project. It is good if major projects can be done in stages that can be built on at a later point, while still being useful even if there is never additional funding for the project. Subsequent phases of the project can be undertaken as funding becomes available and as it is clear that there still is a need for this.

Estimates for construction projects need to be carefully put together by experts. Some funds will obviously be needed up front for architectural fees, for legal documentation and for the purchase of materials. However, for ongoing payments there should be an agreed-upon plan. Credible contractors will provide construction flow-charts that allow progress to be observed against a timetable. Specific funds will only be needed as stages are successfully completed. It may be wise to designate someone who is "yours" to closely monitor every aspect of a building project.

While there are many reasons why projects can cost more than original estimates, legitimate contractors will know how to control what they spend. It is normal to build an extra 10 percent into the construction budget for contingencies, though changes that become necessary during the construction process should be handled in accordance with the agreement made before the construction ever began. One should not start until these things are clear. It is also normal to retain about 5 percent of a final payment until one is satisfied that everything has been done in accordance with what was agreed upon.

One important thing to remember is that as the project is underway all donors need to be receiving photographs and regular reports of the progress. That includes an explanation of all income and expenses for the project (not just their contributions). Should donors choose to visit your project, you don't want them to discover surprises. And when a project is completed, invite the entire community to publicly celebrate everything that you finish!

Conclusions

If we have done a careful job in developing a strategic plan, it is easier to evaluate the use and development of our facilities. We will find ways to maximize what we have, and we will only build or rebuild that which will realistically enhance the quality and effectiveness of our program. Although we should lovingly care for what we have, there is something wrong if we have more pride in our facilities than in our graduates. Our facilities are only one of the resources that we have to carry out our task of equipping students for ministry.

Discussion Questions Regarding Your Facilities

1. Does your strategic plan give you an adequate understanding of how much space and what kind of space you need now? Do you know how much space you are likely to need within five years, and what you might need 10+ years from now?
2. To what extent would restructuring or remodeling existing buildings solve current or future needs?
3. Do you have a site plan? A maintenance plan and a maintenance budget?
4. How do other people perceive you when they look at the facilities that you have?

9

Excellence in Libraries

An excellent library is systematically collected according to a selection policy built on the mission statement of the library and of the school. Trained personnel organize it for maximum usefulness to both students and faculty. The good libraries of the future will not be built on printed materials alone, but will take full advantage of information available globally through information technology.

A library should be one of the most important resources that a theological institution has. It also may be its most expensive facility. Theological education programs require libraries that are both useful and used. The library makes available the materials that students and teachers need for the courses offered. It is a place of research to allow students to gain perspective from what others have thought, along with illustrations, samples and models of what others have done. Archives and other historical records stored in the library help us remember our history. The library should contain up-to-date reference and resource tools, such as dictionaries, encyclopedias, atlases, commentaries and language tools. It needs to receive and keep magazines, newspapers and professional journals.

Yet for much of the non-Western world, libraries are not treated as important aspects of the educational process. Students (and many teachers) may not know how to use a library. The library has little budget and its collection is often made up of donated books, old dictionaries and commentaries. No one uses it other than during the prescribed hours when it becomes a study hall for students to read the multiple copies of textbooks kept there.

One of our biggest needs, even before we try to strengthen the library collection, is to help students and staff to understand what a library is and how it can be used to make training programs excellent. Our library staff also needs to learn how to better serve our teachers, students and staff. And teachers and students need regular orientation as to how to take advantage of our library so as to support the excellence of our training program.

In this chapter we will look at what a library is and how we can strengthen its collection and staff. We also want to consider how we may be able to help in the development of other libraries, including that of our own students.

What Is a Library?

A library is a collection of books and other materials organized for use. This definition has several key words:

1. A library is a collection, not an accumulation. We should not be impressed merely by the number of books on a library's shelves. What matters is that each item is there because of what it contributes to the whole. A copy of Richard Nixon's campaign biography from the 1972 US election contributes absolutely nothing to your theological collection. In order to collect, instead of simply accumulating, we need to know what kinds of materials are needed to support the courses offered to our students. We also need to be aware of what materials exist and what kind of budget we have in order to carefully prioritize what materials can be acquired to strengthen our collection.

2. A library includes materials, not just books. It should also have magazines and periodicals that relate to the social or political realities of the region as well as professional journals in areas that the curriculum covers, such as biblical studies, missions, practical theology or education. A library will likely have videos or audio-visual materials, such as sermons or documentaries, that provide background or illustrations for course offerings. Libraries increasingly should have electronic tools and searchable CDs that allow students and faculty to access an almost incomprehensible amount of research materials through the Internet. A library could also have archival materials to help us remember the history of the school, church denominations or Christian organizations in the region.

3. A library is organized. Its materials are not merely crowded onto shelves. It could be organized by broad categories like Bible, missions or pastoral counseling, or by using detailed systems like the Dewey Decimal Classification, the Library of Congress or the Universal Decimal System. The goal is to organize the materials so they can be found, so don't complicate your system!

4. A library is to be used. In the Middle Ages handwritten manuscripts were chained to desks or locked in trunks in order to preserve them. While you may have precious historical documents that need protection, for most of your collection the goal is that the materials be used, not protected. The location of a library, its hours of use and the system designed for borrowing books should be based on how materials can best be made available for the use of students and faculty – not on what might be most convenient for the library's staff.

Building the Library Collection

A library with 20,000 irrelevant or outdated books is far less useful than a library with 2,000 carefully selected titles. A library should have a selection policy with priorities for what will or will not go into the collection. You also should have a weeding policy to eliminate what should not be there. Not every donation is worth putting on our shelves. Neither will we be able to purchase every book or journal that we want. Choices must be made according to well-considered priorities.

A selection policy should have the input of lots of people and once formulated, it should have official approval by the administration and faculty. It needs to consider the following questions:

- Who will benefit from the library? Only students? Faculty preparing for their classes? Graduate students needing to do specialized advanced research? Pastors and lay leaders from the region? The general public?
- Who has the authority to make decisions about whether a gift should be accepted or a book purchased?
- What process will be followed for the library staff to know what materials are needed to support the courses being offered?

The Librarians' Manual is an excellent tool that has been developed by the Association of Christian Librarians' Commission for International Library Assistance (CILA, http://www.acl.org/cila.cfm). This manual suggests the following guidelines for a selection policy:

   a. Top priority should be given to materials which are most necessary for regular use in the present curriculum and for planned future development of new courses.
   b. Students need books written in non-technical, age-appropriate language, to supplement standard textbooks or class notes.
   c. Teachers need materials that cover the subject matter in greater depth. By maintaining a balance between the purchase of proven classics, primary literature, and up-to-date texts or secondary information, your collection should primarily support the curriculum.
   d. A reasonable balance in the number of materials bought for each subject should be maintained.
   e. Generally, standard textbooks should not be considered for purchase [for the library]. Often textbooks are quite costly and become quickly outdated. . . .[1]

It is not ideal if the library is the primary place for students to have access to their textbooks. It is better if students can acquire their own copies of the books they are studying. This helps them to begin building their own libraries, which for many may be the only library to which they have access for the rest of their ministry lives.

Your teachers are the best source of suggestions about books and materials that are needed in the library, although the reality of budgetary issues and the need for a balanced collection mean that we may not be able to buy everything they ask for. Part of a library's budget must be used to maintain an up-to-date collection of professional journals and magazines that will support the classes being taught and the teachers who teach them. Funds will also be needed for the purchase of expensive reference materials, especially electronic versions. The good news is that some journals or reference materials may not need to

---

1. LeAnne Hardy, Linda Lambert, and Ferne Weimer, *The Librarian's Manual, Revised and Expanded Edition* (Cedarville, OH: ACL, 2008), 33.

be purchased at all, as good materials are increasingly becoming available for free on the Internet. The key issue for all of these things is the size of your library's budget, and you should not quietly acquiesce if this number is ridiculously low! Accreditation agencies usually require a set number of books for accreditation. They also want to see that a reasonable part of the program's operational budget (at least 3 percent in most cases) is designated for library purchases.

Very few of the unsolicited books sent from overseas will be of much use to your library. They may even become more expensive to receive than they are worth if they can't be processed as duty-free or duty-reduced items. It is much better for someone to send you a list of books from which you can select those which will actually be helpful. Items that are in poor condition shouldn't even be offered. It should also be understood that all donations will either be integrated into the exiting collection, shared with another library or sold.

There are a variety of ways in which to learn about what might be useful to have in your library collection. The starting point is to listen to the suggestions of teachers as they develop their bibliographies for their classes. We may also drool over what is advertised in publishers' catalogs, though the reality of limited funds for book purchases suggests that it is wise to only make selections after knowing a book's quality through reading book reviews. It can be helpful to visit other people's libraries to see what they have (especially in journals). You will also discover books that need to be purchased again as you do an annual inventory of your entire collection to see what might be missing (or completely worn out). If you choose to remove a book from the collection, the information on that book should be removed from the catalog.

Your library staff will need to maintain four separate lists:

1. A wish list of books that you hope to acquire as funds become available
2. A list of books ready to be ordered
3. A list of books that have already been ordered (so that you don't inadvertently order them again during the months while you are waiting for them to come)

4. A list of books that have been received and are being processed, but which aren't yet on the shelves (to let impatient professors know that what they need is almost ready).

It can be very beneficial to be part of a consortium with a Catholic school or a secular university. Your library will include a good collection of evangelical titles that you can share with them. They will hopefully have everything else which they will be willing to share with you. You can either allow other students or faculty to use your facilities, with your students having the right to their library, or you could develop a system of inter-library loans.

A library collection can grow exponentially as it acquires the equipment (and the expertise) to allow it to take advantage of the massive amount of research information and articles available through information technology. Students will need help in sorting through the quality of what they find. Bibliographic research can be done online, with certain books and journals available for free. Full access to the collections of other schools is not yet a reality, although there are a variety of projects to digitize just about anything.[2]

So perhaps there is hope for multiplying our collections in the relatively near future. Electronic subscription services for journals may be costly, but can be worth the price if they allow for access to a number of periodicals that could be useful to students and teachers.

Library Facilities

In the same way that men who don't cook shouldn't design kitchens, deciding how to build and design a library is not a task that should be left to teachers, administrators or architects. You need the help of a trained librarian to create a functional library. Ask for help if you are considering building a library or re-designing the one that you have, especially if you don't already have a trained librarian!

An excellent library facility needs to have comfortable and adequate space for all the activities that will be connected with the library. For security reasons, there should be only one main entrance to the library collection (with emergency exits, of course). The circulation desk should be located at

---

2. See for example: https://books.google.com/ or http://scholar.google.com/.)

that entrance so that materials can be returned easily and so that nothing can be removed from the library without checking it out properly.

As the library's catalog is where most research begins, it should also be located near the main entrance, which means that it will also be near to where someone could answer questions. If you have an electronic catalog, make sure that it is user friendly and that you have access to good local technical support. Reserved reading material also should be located somewhere near the front desk, though popular periodicals and newspapers may be placed where people can sit and talk without disturbing others. A library needs a separate room for work space with lots of shelves for supplies and for books to be processed or repaired.

Books need to be on the shelves and available to students. To allow your collection to grow, books probably shouldn't take up more than approximately 70 percent of any given shelf. Contrary to popular belief most books don't disappear, though they can seem to if they have been misfiled on a shelf. It is better to let someone who knows what they are doing reshelf books that have been used.

If a library contains computers, and especially if the computers are connected to the Internet, you will need a secure place to keep them with a password system that will control who has access to the Internet. (You may also want a control system to block access to inappropriate websites.) Heat and humidity can reduce the life of a computer by as much as a third, so the costs of installing and running air conditioning may be less than the cost of replacing computers that wear out faster than they need to.

All libraries need adequate lighting and to find ways to dampen echoes and noise. If at all possible, a library should have an air-flow system to control dust and humidity. Both of these are very hard on your books, so the cost of installing, running and maintaining a climate-control system is off-set by the reduced cost of having to replace materials.

How much study space is needed in a library depends on many factors. It is helpful for upper-level students to have their own semi-private space for their research. For everyone else, how much study space you need will depend on usage. If all students are required to do their homework in the library at the same times, you will obviously need space for tables and chairs to accommodate every single one of them. However, if you don't have this kind of required study hall, you will need to conduct a survey to get a sense of library usage and plan accordingly. Some students don't have study space at home and may study in the library even if it isn't required. Have enough space so that your library doesn't feel crowded.

Library Personnel

Libraries should be run and managed by people who know what they are doing. People who work in libraries tend to be either those who love books and know theology well, but who need help in learning library organizational skills – or those who have received technical training in library management, but who don't know much about the kinds of books found in a theological training program. The ideal librarian is trained and skilled in both areas. If your librarian has a degree in library science, it can be helpful to allow him or her to audit classes or to even work towards a degree in theology. If your librarian is a seminary graduate, it will be to your advantage to encourage his or her training in library management. Formal library training can be obtained through many local universities in the non-Western world, or through distance education options. You can also encourage your librarian to participate in workshops or to obtain supervision from trained librarians at larger regional schools or from local university libraries.

Not all libraries will be able to afford a full-time librarian with a library degree, though you may have concluded that your library is important enough for you to try to afford one. It is not unreasonable to reserve a full 10 percent of your operational budget towards having a good library collection, hiring an adequate library staff, and having a climate-controlled facility with good equipment.

Several schools could opt to share a professional librarian who will train and monitor the staff doing the day-to-day maintenance of each of the libraries. Although there are online systems that can help with book classification, you still want expertise to process or purchase your books. Books can be bought with "cataloging in publication" (CIP), but it needs to be verified that the CIP fits with the classification system you use in your library. Trained short-term volunteers may be able to help you with projects like this.

How to Help Those Who Don't (or Won't) Have Easy Access to a Library

As important as libraries are to helping our students grow and learn, it may be that our invisible curriculum has "taught" them that learning is only possible through listening to experts in class and by going to a library to read what has been assigned. A teacher can also communicate that if something isn't said by an expert, or if it can't be footnoted from a printed book, it probably isn't true. So since many of our students may never attend another formal class and since they probably won't have access to a library after they graduate, the invisible curriculum has taught them that their days of learning may soon be over.

We need a teaching methodology that helps students understand that there are many ways to learn and to do research. While we want them to develop a love for learning from books, they also need to learn from the insights of others as well as to value their own field research as this is what will help them know what to preach each week.

There may be several ways in which we can help with the development of a variety of "libraries."

1. Personal libraries for students. Each student should begin to acquire his or her own library, built around the key textbooks and basic reference materials. These will allow a student to review and to re-teach what has been learned in school.

2. Mini-libraries in churches. As an institution, we could develop special cooperative projects as part of our ongoing commitment to our graduates, to allow them to develop libraries in the churches where they go to serve. As they teach and train their own people, they will be able to help their people learn from written materials.

3. Basic libraries for study centers. Extension training programs (which we will discuss in chapter 11) will need to have basic libraries for those students who study at or through these study centers. It might be possible to loan books to the extension center for a particular course, or to develop CDs or electronic materials that support the extension training that we are offering.

4. Electronic materials. If we develop extension training materials for the Internet, we will need to discover how we can make the reading requirements for our courses available on a website or through CDs.

Conclusions

For many faculty members who return from overseas study, what they miss most is the libraries that they used. May you be able to develop the kind of library that will not only serve your program excellently, but which will make your graduates homesick as well!

Discussion Questions Regarding Your Library

1. To what extent do faculty and students know how to use your library effectively?
2. Is your library collection adequate? Do you have both a selection policy and a weeding policy that work? Why or why not?
3. How adequate are your library facilities and staff? Do you have, or have access to, the expertise you need for developing an excellent library?
4. Are there ways that you could develop a library consortium with others so that you better share the resources that you all have?
5. How could you find more financial resources to improve your library?
6. To what extent are you ready for what technology will do to the way libraries are configured and used?
7. How could you help your students and graduates – and their respective ministries – develop their own libraries?

Website Suggestions for Further Study

The Librarian's Manual order form: http://www.acl.org/librariansmanual orderform.cfm
Dewey Decimal Classification System order form: http://www.oclc.org/dewey/
Library of Congress Catalog: http://www.loc.gov/index.html <library catalogs>
   Shows the LC classification for any book published in America.

Library of Congress classification tables and subject headings order form: http://www.loc.gov/cds/

Sears List of Subject Headings ordering: http://www.hwwilson.com/print/searslst18th.cfm for ordering

Suggestions for Further Reading

Hardy, LeAnne, Linda Lambert, and Ferne Weimer. *The Librarian's Manual, Revised and Expanded Edition* (Cedarville, OH: ACL, 2008).

Moreau, A. Scott, and Mike O'Rear. "Browsing Virtual Libraries and Book Collections." *Evangelical Mission Quarterly* 42, no. 2 (2006): 254–259.

10

Excellence in Fundraising

An excellent leadership training institution is adequately funded to do what the strategic plan says should be done. It takes responsibility for its financial health and builds self-reliance. An excellent program maintains good relationships with its friends, churches and ministries, and especially with its students once they graduate. It benefits from healthy partnerships, especially with those who claim it as their training program.

Leadership training is strategic kingdom work, equipping God's people for ministry, for the growth and strengthening of the church. Hudson Taylor said that "God's work, done in God's way, will never lack for supplies." Yet the vast majority of training institutions seem to lack a lot of things. Why? How can we become stronger financially?

In this chapter we want to consider the financing of theological education institutions. Given the importance of leadership training for the health of the church, we need to examine the reasons why so many institutions struggle in the area of finances. What motivates people to give, or hinders them from giving? Financial health does not happen solely through increasing the number of overseas donors. Neither are we likely to solve everything through local donor sources, increased tuition or managing income-generating projects. Fund development requires work, using a variety of creative efforts, building on relationships that we have or could have.

Why Do We Struggle to Have Enough?

The vast majority of theological training programs are far from being well-funded. There are many good and bad reasons for this. Not all of these reflect your situation, but let us consider some of why training programs may struggle financially.

We Need to Learn Spiritual Dependence

Those who have everything can find it difficult to depend on God. If our financial bases are completely covered, we tend to forget who it is that really owns all that we have. It is important to develop budgets and manage our resources well. But it is also good to need to pray daily for our bread, along with our health, safety, salaries and electric bills. This is what it means to seek first the kingdom of God (Matt 6:33). As students join in praying for our daily survival, presenting our needs to God and giving thanks for all that he provides, we are teaching lifetime lessons about what it means to be in Christ, in whom "we live and move and have our being" (Acts 17:28). God is aware of what we need. As we should have learned from those who wandered for forty years in the desert, we need less complaining and a lot more prayer.

Some May Have Done Too Much

I doubt that Bible school leaders consciously build monuments for their own glory (or to acknowledge the egos of their donors), but it may seem that way to others. Funding that could have helped buy textbooks or pay better salaries was spent for projects that didn't need to be done, or at least not at the scale at which they were done. Even if specially designated funds were given for the initial project, the institution is now struggling as it uses its limited operational budget to maintain or furnish what was built so that it can be used at all. Local churches and friends may look at the magnificent buildings and conclude that the school no longer needs their financial help, since it obviously has an abundance from other sources.

There Can Be Misunderstandings or Power Struggles over Finances

Salaries for teachers and staff at a Bible school may be lower than what is paid to local university or secondary school teachers, yet significantly higher than what is paid to denominational leaders or local pastors. Staff housing and student dormitories may be nicer than what many local pastors have. Campus buildings or the school's chapel may be bigger and better furnished than denominational offices or local churches. Jealousies arise, along with struggles over who controls finances that come from overseas. Access to foreign funding for operations can also be a disincentive to contributions from local sources, especially when people imagine that there is a lot more coming in than there really is.

Resources May Not Be Managed Well

There are many ways to contribute to one's own poverty. This includes both administrative disorganization and mismanagement of funds. Theological programs are not exempt from employees who walk off with money or supplies. We need regular audits and institutional controls over who can spend our funds and how. All payments should be made from an approved budget, with appropriate authorizations and receipts, rather than working from the petty cash box to cover what seems most urgent today. When designated funds can be easily "borrowed" to pay bills that seem more pressing, serious issues of credibility are raised with those who gave the designated funds. Donors may become disillusioned and decide never to entrust the school with anything more.

Training institutions often have overly complicated financial systems. There aren't simple ways to make financial decisions. Salaries or financial records can be months in arrears. If there are receipts, they get loosely thrown into desk drawers to be organized only occasionally. Vehicles, equipment and supplies can be used a bit too freely for personal reasons. Meetings are held in restaurants or travel is done without much consideration as to whether the school can afford it. No one negotiates between competitors or does comparison shopping for better prices or for better bank rates. While these things may seem trivial, the end result of administrative inefficiency is an accumulation of expenses for which there won't be funds. Administration is not a gift automatically found in either pastors or teachers so it may be worth asking someone with skills in organizational management to help you find simpler ways to manage the resources that you have.

The Program Is Overstaffed for the Number of Students That It Has

Too few students tends to mean a shortage of operational funds. Perhaps some painful decisions need to be made about releasing workers that the program can't afford. However, there may be other problems as well. Low student enrollment may indicate that the program isn't meeting the felt needs of churches and the community. Do students and churches even know that you exist? There may be many potential students who would love to study in your program if only they knew about you. Or are you competing in a market saturated with training programs? There is no point in trying to run a program that isn't needed.

The Employees Are Paid Too Much

This is really unlikely, although in schools without governing boards or systems of financial control, a handful of leaders may establish unrealistic salary packages for themselves.

Tuition Fees Are Too Low

We may feel that if we raise our fees, we will lose most of our students to programs that are "cheaper." The reality is that offering free or cheap education is not the way to attract the best students, since people normally do not value something that costs little or nothing. It is important to communicate the actual costs of educating a student (total operational costs, including volunteer help, divided by the number of students). Rather than lowering fees, we need friends who can provide scholarships or help subsidize our overall operational costs.

The Program Is Not Viable

Many Bible schools were created during colonial days by mission organizations that staffed and funded them. In time, titles and ownership were transitioned to national churches or to the school itself. However, what was developed by mission organizations is beyond the national church's ability to fund or maintain without missionaries and mission funding. If your training institution were to be recreated from scratch today, you might well exist in a different location and with vastly different structure so as to be more affordable and culturally relevant. Trying to maintain what was inherited from a different era may be too heavy a burden to carry.

There Is Not a Broad Enough Ownership of the Training Program

Local churches may never have felt that this was their program. Even if they do, when they struggle to pay their own pastors, they feel that they couldn't possibly contribute anything to help the school. Maybe they were never taught to give, as the invisible curriculum of the colonial days convinced them that they were too poor to share their resources. Or perhaps they simply think that schools already have adequate funding from other sources.

Not Enough People Were Asked to Help

Many theological training programs don't do a good job of internal or external communication about how God is using them. No one knows that the school even has needs. Most teachers and administrators would rather not do public relations or raise funds, even though there may be many local churches, businessmen, foundations and alumni who would happily contribute to scholarships, special projects or operational expenses if only someone asked them. As we discussed in chapter 5, healthy administrative structures have a team to do this, headed by a vice-president of public relations and fundraising. We may not have one because we aren't well structured to do the asking.

Developing a Fundraising Strategy

A fundraising strategy should arise directly from your strategic plan. We need to fund that which needs to be done. We should not be donor driven, doing only those projects that a donor wants to fund. From the strategic plan, we already know what needs to be funded. A fundraising strategy involves discovering who might be interested in becoming a part of your support team and reflecting on how these people should be approached.

The place to start is with yourselves. If you won't contribute to your cause, why should anyone else want to contribute to it? Our best fundraising ideas will come as our advisory board, governing council, students, faculty and staff prayerfully and creatively consider ways to discover the financial resources that we need. Most of those who become a part of this support team will come from the school's network of relationships and partners. Thus, who are those from our family, friends, churches, business friends, friends of friends, etc., who could be asked to join us in supporting our educational ministry?

As we mentioned in chapter 5, there should be a competent executive-level leader on the administrative staff team to coordinate public relations and fundraising efforts. Teachers are probably not the best ones to write the school's newsletters. It takes conscious effort and time to build bridges and to establish credibility with businesses, foundations, Christian organizations or key individuals who might be willing to provide funding for your program. You should have a team of people with communication skills in public relations who will be able to communicate the successes and needs of your program to others and to build healthy partnerships.

We want strong financial supporters who will keep on giving to our programs. But what might motivate a person to consider supporting a ministry like ours? What might hinder some people from wanting to help?

Motivations for Giving

Hopefully people will enthusiastically want to become financial supporters as they learn about your vision and see what God is doing through you. However, some people are simply unaware of their responsibility to be stewards of God's resources (Matt 25:14–30), to use what they have for the good of others, and not just for serving themselves (Mark 10:45). God blesses us so that we can be a blessing to others (1 Cor 9:11–14). Though Christ was "rich, yet for [our] sakes he became poor, so that [we] though his poverty might become rich" (2 Cor 8:9). One's riches may not include lots of cash, but believers have been made rich "in every way" so that their "generosity will result in thanksgiving to God" (2 Cor 9:11). Jesus was God's gift to us (2 Cor 9:15) and giving should be an expression of thanksgiving to God for all that he has done for us.

Few Christians in the non-Western world have been taught about giving. Perhaps your training institution could develop seminars for local churches to help Christians understand some basic principles of stewardship. Paul wrote "Command them to do good, to be rich in good deeds and to be generous and willing to share" (1 Tim 6:18).

However, we should not motivate giving by provoking guilt or by promising people special honors or rewards as a result of their giving. Dr Manfred W. Kohl made a strong statement at a conference at the Oxford Centre for Mission Studies in 1995: "Giving, sharing and commitment are neither means to, nor a sign of, spirituality. Nor are they merits which qualify one to be numbered among God's redeemed people." Our giving should be done cheerfully, voluntarily, eagerly and generously (2 Cor 8:2–4; 9:5, 7).

Obstacles to Giving

Why do some people opt to not help you financially? Do they assume that you already have enough? Are they unaware of your needs? Or are there serious issues of credibility that have made them, their churches or others unwilling to help you at all? People need to have confidence in who we are and what we are doing. Are they aware of your core values and do they know enough of your track record to see that you practice what you preach? You need to discover if there are problems that have led to a lack of trust in you and your work. Building a good reputation is not easy and we need God's help and grace to protect us from rumors and stories that simply aren't true.

Some donors give only once. Why don't they give a second time? It takes a lot of effort to discover new people, so how can we keep donors, once we discover them? The key comes in strong personal relationships, along with good reporting. Donors need to know that their gifts have been used, as was intended, for well-planned strategic projects. People don't want to feel pressured or manipulated. But they do appreciate being invited to participate in something worth doing, and then seeing the results of their gift. They like options, so it can help to offer several projects that need financial assistance. People also like to give to what others are giving to, so we need to be as transparent as we can about the financial assistance that we receive from others.

It is the job of your development team to stay in touch with people and organizations that are interested (or who should be interested!) in what you are doing. We need to keep them informed about us and then have the courage to ask for help when we need it.

Does the Solution Come from Overseas?

From their very first days, many mission-created schools have been highly dependent on foreign personnel and foreign funding. For such training institutions, financial survival is found only with regular and significant funding from overseas organizations. However, not all of these so-called partnerships are healthy, and this is not the best way to secure financial stability. There can often be serious problems when one donor source is providing most of the funding. There is no real partnership if you are functionally working for me. Despite our friendship or all my reassuring words to the contrary, it will be hard for you not to feel pressured or manipulated if you sense that by not doing what I want, you may no longer receive my blessing. That's especially awkward if I am the one who is providing most of your operational funds, program grants, faculty support and scholarship assistance. It is better to have financial support coming from a number of different sources. However, even when no one source is dominant, funding from overseas often comes with strings attached by people who may know very little about local realities.

Should Most Funding Be Raised Locally?

Local funding should be a significant part of a school's income as this reflects satisfaction with the impact that the training program has. Realistic tuition fees allow every student to contribute something towards his or her own training, with their families and churches happily investing in those they know and believe in. Graduates of the program should offer gifts of thanksgiving for what they received during their studies. Churches that have received these graduates should offer gifts of thanksgiving to reflect their satisfaction with the competence of the pastors and leaders that they now have. The business community should be delighted to invest in the development of people with character and quality leadership skills. Local foundations can help with projects that have local impact. We ourselves should invest in our own program.

For most training institutions in the non-Western world, tuition is much too low. However, being self-reliant does not mean that *all* operational funds should come from internal tuition or fees. As I reviewed financial statements from Christian colleges in North America, only about a third of their operational income is from student tuition. The remainder comes from foundation grants and donations from alumni and friends of the school. Neither does being self-reliant indicate that all of their income was generated locally or within a particular geographic area. These colleges and universities apparently will take (and seek) funds from wherever they can be found.

Theological training institutions in the non-Western world do not need to be different. The fundamental issue is not where the funds come from. A training institution becomes self-sufficient when it takes responsibility for raising and administering its own funds. Many should be invited to help you with the work that God has called you to do. With the exception of those denominational programs that function under the budget of the denomination, no one source should provide more than 50 percent of a school's operational funds. More than this gives a donor too much potential control over the program, as well as putting the program at risk if funding were to be withdrawn.

Income-Generating Projects

Theological training programs need to think creatively about a variety of ways that they can generate income for their training efforts. A program in India has developed a major conference center to host both secular and Christian groups. A program in South Africa had some extra office space and empty faculty housing and fixed it up to be leased to several other Christian organizations. A campus in Brazil is rented out during vacation or holiday times to host conferences or workshops. A variety of training programs have agricultural projects to raise chickens or vegetables to be sold at a profit, or to be eaten by the staff and students. A program in Brazil offers most of its program's classes in the evening, and then uses the facility as a community school during the day to generate income. Workshops or seminars could be offered for a fee by the school's staff as part of professional leadership development for the community in areas like leadership, strategic planning, chaplaincy, counseling or conflict resolution. A Middle Eastern program makes some income by using the Bible to train non-Christian tour guides. A Brazilian program generates income by using one corner of its campus and some of its foreign staff and families to offer English classes to young people in the community, etc.

However, there are at least four dangers related to income-generating projects.

1. Projects can become a distraction to the training side of a training program, as they can require energy, people and finances that would more appropriately be used elsewhere.
2. Projects are often ineptly led by people without managerial or business skills.
3. Many projects were someone's spontaneous good idea launched with minimal market research to verify that there was a felt need for the project.
4. A project may become a "white elephant," something that actually consumes more resources than it generates.

The only justification for having an income-generating project is to provide income for the school. It is not our core business to run businesses. As we discussed in chapter 5, we should not take on unnecessary administration. Each income-generating project must have its own set of financial books with its own management and staff team. Running a project should not require time from the school's leadership, other than to verify with the project's governing body that what is being done is actually worth the trouble.

Financial Support from Relationships

Our primary financial supporters are those who consider us to be their school. This is part of ownership as they work with us to achieve financial viability and stability. Who should these partners be and how can we strengthen our partnership with them?

Alumni

One very important partnership should be with our graduates. These former students are hopefully satisfied with the training they received. All students should get a glimpse of the many partners who are helping to underwrite the real costs of their training. From their very first days as students, they should be challenged to commit themselves over a lifetime to continue to make this kind of training available for others. Each graduate should be encouraged to offer yearly gifts of thanksgiving to the Lord for what they have received from the school. As God blesses them in special ways, they can give to special projects, such as books for the library or construction or remodeling projects.

Every training program needs to regularly be in touch with its graduates. The development team should maintain an up-to-date mailing and emailing list. However, our graduates need to feel that they are more than just potential sources of funding. They will be our primary recruiters of new students. And as we will note in chapter 12, our alumni are one of our best sources for feedback to help us improve what we are doing.

We can offer our graduates seminars and workshops on topics that will sharpen their ministry skills. We can strengthen their relationships with other graduates as they are all invited back to campus at least once a year for celebrations of special events, such as graduation or a week of spiritual emphasis. Share stories with them about what God continues to do at their school. Give them news about their colleagues and specific ways that they can pray for one another and for the training program. As our alumni continue to be excited about what we are doing, they will be open to contribute financially to us (although we will still need to ask).

Mission Organizations

Another important partnership will be with your founding mission organization. Founding missions usually continue to contribute much to the theological education programs they helped to start. They know your history and can give good advice. They can use their network of contacts to raise funds for special projects for construction or equipment. Mission organizations can offer scholarships for students that serve the churches they work with, or assist with the salary of a national teacher or staff member. They often provide missionaries to serve on the faculty and staff.

All of these things can be very helpful, though there are some gentle steps that we need to take to make sure that this is a healthy partnership. As we mentioned earlier, all teachers, including missionaries, need to be evaluated before they are accepted (with a contract) as part of our teaching or administrative team. Not every missionary necessarily has the cross-cultural or communication skills that we need. We may sense that there could be problems with lifestyles or attitudes that would hinder a person from fitting in well.

Mission organizations, like everyone else, are free to dream with us about the future. However, founding missions need to remember that they are no longer in charge of every project. As we discussed in chapter 5, there should be a track record of excellence in administration so that mission organizations can trust the school to use funds for the projects for which they were given. Thus, their fundraising should be limited to projects that have been approved by the school. Salaries or benefits for national staff should not be paid by the mission directly to individuals, as this can create jealousies (others assume that they are receiving a lot more than they really are) and confusion (does the individual work for the mission or for the school?)

It is not easy to transition control. It is awkward when a father retires from the business he started, but then shows up every day to watch his son work, or when a pastor retires after many years in a church, but stays on as a member of the church. The difference is that the mission hasn't retired, it just voluntarily passed on the chairmanship. Being in charge is a hard habit to change. So while one wants to honor them and to continue to hear what they have to say, we (and they) need to remember that it is our school to manage.

A training institution helps itself with this if it has a multiplicity of donor sources. This also makes it easier for a founding mission to say yes – or no – without feeling that they are dominating or manipulating. There is an appropriate place to share their opinions if they are thoroughly integrated into the general assembly, along with the other organizations and churches that provide faculty, students or funding. No one person or organization should have more influence over us than all others. The proper forum for discussing ideas and making recommendations is at the general assembly or as a member of the governing board, not while holding the checkbook in the principal's office.

Christian Organizations

A training institution may also have partnerships with several Christian organizations. Not only are our graduates working with them, but we may discover ways to be of service to them. In asking, "How can we help you?" we need to evaluate whether our basic mission and purpose, and the resources that we have, allow us to respond to their needs.

Their side of the partnership will certainly include paying for the tuition of their students, though there may be other creative ways to partner as well. For example, SIL/ Wycliffe designated several upper-level regional institutions for training their translation consultants. Besides raising funds for the tuition and board of the students they send, they have provided several teachers with specialized skills in Bible translation along with technical books for the library to support their part of the school's curriculum. Trans-World Radio has partnered with several training institutions to construct radio facilities on their campuses. TWR staff help with teaching and give occasional seminars to train students (and faculty) in how to develop radio programming and how radio can enhance their ministries. World Vision partnered with several training programs to develop a leadership training curriculum for its many staff around the world. They helped with funding and provided teachers for a program that served not only their own employees, but others as well.

Local Churches

As we discussed in chapter 4, our owners are those churches and denominations that consider us to be their training institution. Our mission is to prepare their students to be effective leaders and pastors. These churches are hopefully active in our general assembly. Part of our partnership with them should be to send our faculty, staff and students to visit them and listen to them, as well as to minister in their churches. They should receive regular information about us that includes stories about what God is doing in and through us. They need to be aware of ways they can pray for us. They also need to understand our financial needs.

The primary responsibility of churches should be to support those that they have sent for study. They may complain that they have absolutely no funds for this, yet somehow somebody would have managed to house and feed these students if they hadn't come to study at all. So it is not true that there is nothing available for their students. Perhaps they could send food instead of money. But if a church is unwilling to invest anything in its own students, then we should be reticent to help them as well.

The denominations that you serve should be asked to add your training program to their budget since you are training leaders and pastors for them. The annual conference or churches within a denomination could schedule a special time of celebration once a year with an offering to provide books or scholarships for students. Churches that have received your graduates should be encouraged to offer yearly gifts that reflect their satisfaction with the kind of pastor and leader that they have received from you.

Foundations

Foundations are found throughout the world, including locally. They may be created with family wealth or from profits from a business. There are also public foundations. What they all have in common is their purpose to give away funds for specific causes that interest them. Even mission organizations can be treated like foundations as they can be asked for specific help with specific projects. There are three important steps in developing a healthy partnership with a foundation.

1. You need to discover who has an interest in what you are trying to do. You can begin to research this through websites that list foundations and the various causes they support. I have attached some of these at the end of this chapter. The overwhelming majority of foundations are not interested in theological education, or in your part of the world. But some might be, or they might be interested in some aspect of what you are doing. For example, if they have an interest in the leadership development of women in the non-Western world, you could ask for scholarship help for your female students or for faculty assistance for women on your staff team. If their interest is HIV/AIDS, you could request a grant to buy materials for your library, or to enable you to offer a workshop on issues related to AIDS to teachers and students. Begin by doing your homework, including learning from other training programs about foundations that have shown interest in them.

2. It takes time to develop a relationship with a foundation. It is usually better to write them and ask if they would be willing to look at a project than to spend funds to visit them or to start by sending them a full project proposal. Even those that do agree to consider your projects will probably say no to your initial request. There are lots of reasons why foundations and organizations say no. They may not have adequate funds for this year, or

they may feel that they don't yet know you well enough. But as you have an opportunity to help them get to know you, and as they hear from others about you (foundations routinely recommend projects to other foundations), a relationship can begin. After several requests, they may offer a small grant. If they are satisfied with how you use the grant, they may choose to invest in you again.

3. There's a lot of paperwork involved in relating to foundations. It is absolutely correct to be accountable for the gifts we receive. Furthermore, our requests should be written with quality and clarity as we explain how our projects will contribute to the overall objectives of our program. I have attached an appendix describing what should be included in a project proposal for a foundation. We should also provide all donors with well-written financial and performance reports on what was accomplished with their gifts.

Some foundations seem to ask for more paperwork than their donations are worth. It is acceptable to disengage, but do so graciously, remembering that foundations talk to each other.

The Business Community/Government Assistance

There is a need for quality Christian leaders in the marketplace. This is not the main focus of most theological training programs, though it should be the primary purpose of Christian colleges and universities that are increasingly being developed throughout the non-Western world. Nevertheless, the primary influencers for change in many places continue to be pastors and Christian leaders. Both governments and the business community know this. As we develop leaders with solid Christian character, we are doing something that benefits our society. We need to build relationships with key business leaders to help them understand what we are doing. We should challenge Christian business leaders to pray for us and invest in us. We may also be able to take advantage of their wisdom and managerial skills to help us administrate our schools better.

Few schools will be in a hurry to build partnerships with their governments. However, if we are doing a good job of preparing those who serve people, we are performing a useful public function. Our graduates may become the leaders of churches and organizations that respond effectively to social problems. Accordingly, there may be public grants or funding that are available. We need to investigate our options, while carefully considering the strings that may be attached.

Friends of the School

Everyone who ever visits your campus or comes to an event sponsored by your training program should be invited to become a partner with you. Collect their names and addresses, and regularly send them information about what God is doing in and through you. You can invite these people to campus activities (like graduation or special events). Ask them for both prayer support and financial help. Some "friends of the school" have even formed legal corporations to promote the school in their home areas.

You can also be proactive about finding people to come and visit you. Invite North American, European or Australian college students or their churches to enroll in a training module designed for them to understand practices of worship, prayer, church history or contextualized theology. Most visitors will happily cover the costs of these kinds of courses.

Short-term work teams also offer potential new partnerships. Look for small projects for them to do in campus maintenance or in processing library books. Perhaps they can go with some of your students as they do outreach or ministry projects. Their lives will be changed as they get to know you. They will also become ambassadors on your behalf. As your development team stays in touch with them, there may be projects that they, or their churches or institutions, can help with, such as buying books for your library or allowing their faculty or church staff to do modular teaching. Repeat visits and ongoing short-term teams will likely grow into a wonderful partnership.

Conclusions

Excellent theological training institutions take responsibility for their own financial needs. It is good when we remember our dependency on God for everything. But it is also good to remember that God gives to others so that they can graciously and voluntarily take care of God's projects. Start with yourselves and your graduates and build relationships wherever you can find them. If your training program is excellent, and if you have a clear strategic plan to show where you are going and what you need to get there, others should be delighted to invest in what God is doing through you. May God "meet all your needs according to his glorious riches in Christ Jesus" (Phil 4:19).

Discussion Questions Regarding Your Fundraising

1. Why is it that you are struggling financially? Are there areas where you need to change? If so, where and how?
2. Who are your partners? In what sense are these healthy partnerships? How could you build more relationships and strengthen the partnerships that you have?
3. To what extent do you feel controlled by resources managed by your founding mission or by a small handful of financial supporters?
4. How well structured and competent is your development team? Do you have a fundraising strategy? How adequate or effective is it?
5. What creative ideas might you (or your students, your faculty, your staff, your general assembly, etc.) have for generating additional resources for your training program?

Websites on Grantmaking, Fundraising and Foundations

Associated Grantmakers of Massachusetts. www.agmconnect.org/

Charities Aid Foundation: Directory of Grantmaking Trusts (listing the names of over 2,500 trusts). http://www.grant-tracker.org/

The Foundation Center. http://fdncenter.org/ (They also have an extensive list of periodicals on fundraising at http://fdncenter.org/washington/dc_periodicals.html.)

The Grantsmanship Center. www.tgci.com/.

TearFund. "Roots 6 – Fundraising" available at www.tearfund.org/tilz. 100 Church Road, Teddington, TW11 8QE, UK

Suggestions for Further Reading

Jossey-Bass Publications (www.josseybass .com/) has an extensive collection of excellent resources for fund development. They also publish a quarterly journal on issues of philanthropy called *New Directions for Philanthropic Fundraising*. A large listing of books on fundraising or fund-management can be found through www.amazon.com/. There is an incredible lot of material that can be uncovered through the creative use of Google or another search engine. Some specific books that may be useful are:

Burkett, Larry. *Business by the Book: Complete Guide of Biblical Principles for the Workplace*. Nashville, TN: Thomas Nelson, 1998, 2006.

Burnett, Ken. *Relationship Fundraising: A Donor-based Approach to the Business of Raising Money*, 2nd ed. San Francisco, CA: Jossey-Bass, 2002.

Carlson, Mim. *Winning Grants: Step by Step*. 2nd ed. San Francisco, CA: Jossey-Bass, 2002.

Gottlieb, Hildy. *FriendRaising: Community Engagement Strategies for Boards Who Hate Fundraising but Love Making Friends*. Resolve, Inc., D/B/A Renaissance Press, 2000.

Jeavons, Thomas H., and Rebekah Burch Basinger. *Growing Givers' Hearts: Teaching Fundraising as Ministry*. San Francisco, CA: Jossey-Bass, 2000.

Klein, Ken. *Ask and You Shall Receive: A Fundraising Training Program for Religious Organizations*. San Francisco, CA: Jossey-Bass, 2000.

Kohl, Manfred W. "Responsible Stewardship in Theological Education: Guidelines for Resource Development in Post-Communist Countries." *Christian Education Journal* 2 NS, no.1 (Spring 1998): 57–74.

Kutz, John, and Katherine Murray. *Fundraising for Dummies*. Foster City, CA: IDG Books Worldwide, 2000. (www.odgbooks.com. 919 E. Hillsdale Blvd, Suite 400, Foster City, CA, 94404)

New, Cheryl Carter, and James Aaron Quick. *How to Write a Grant Proposal*. San Francisco, CA: Jossey-Bass, 2003.

Nouwen, Henri J. M. *The Spirituality of Fund-Raising*. New York, NY: Henri Nouwen Society, 2004.

Weinstein, Stanley. *The Complete Guide to Fundraising Management*. San Francisco, CA: Jossey-Bass, 2000.

Appendix to Chapter 10

Writing Project Proposals

Whether you are writing to a foundation, a businessman, a mission organization or a secular funding source, every project proposal needs to include the following information:

1. Who are you?

This should indicate the name of your program, your location, legal status, and your purpose, core values and goals. People need to know if you are legitimate and credible, so you will want to demonstrate your competence to do what you are doing, your accreditation status and a bit of your accomplishments. You may want to attach a basic brochure about your program, a list of the names and address of board members, your latest newsletter, the president's report on last year's activities and an audited financial statement.

2. What need will this project help solve?

This is not a description of the project, but an explanation, with data and facts, of the problem that you are responding to. What benefits will be there be for people other than yourselves? Responding to this need must be an obvious extension of your mission and goals.

3. What are the objectives or goals of your project?

This is not a description of what you will do, but of measurable things that the project will accomplish within a particular time frame.

4. How will these goals be achieved?

What must be done and in what sequence to meet your objectives? Why is the methodology that you have chosen appropriate for responding to this need? What staff are needed and what kinds of qualifications do they need to have?

5. How much funding will be needed?

Present realistic details of both the income that you expect to receive for the project and what will be spent and when. These numbers should include the contributions of volunteer help, as well as in-kind gifts.

6. How will the project be evaluated?

How will you know that the objectives have been achieved? Who will do an evaluation and how? Who will receive copies of the final report?

A project proposal needs a one-page "Executive Summary." While inviting the reader to study the supporting documentation that explains everything in greater detail, this summary uses separate paragraphs to simply and clearly answer:

- Who you are,
- The specific purpose of the project for which you are asking for assistance,
- Why you are qualified to do this project,
- What the anticipated results will be within the time frame of the project, and
- How much funding (out of the total project need) you are requesting from them.

You will also need a one-page cover letter on the letterhead of your training institution and addressed to the appropriate contact person. You should briefly explain why you are writing to them, and invite them to read the executive summary and the supporting documents. Say that you will be contacting them within the next two weeks or so, and promise them whatever additional information they might need.[1]

---

1. Adapted from a workshop presented by Dr Manfred W. Kohl at an OCI Institute for Excellence in Budapest in April 2000.

11

Excellence in Extending Training

Excellent training institutions extend their influence and training beyond their campuses. They serve their graduates and the ministries and communities of their graduates in a variety of formal and non-formal ways. They make good use of information technology, both on campus and in their extension efforts.

Most people think of "education" as something done in a specific *place* (with facilities, library, faculty and classrooms) during a specific period of *time* (as an accredited package of courses done at a specific level). The methodology and infrastructures of traditional training programs largely reflect what is done in universities, which were designed as educational packages for pre-career young people. Thanks to the colonial legacy, residential training tends to be the standard against which all programs, including theological training, are measured.

Much of this is changing, both in the secular world and for theological training programs. The educational enterprise has discovered a massive market of adults who might want their services, but who won't (for a variety of reasons) come to its schools as full-time students. Educators have discovered that it is both effective and satisfying to teach people in the context of where they live and work. Adults have questions for which they want answers. They are ready to put lessons immediately into practice.

In this chapter we want to consider how theological training programs can extend their programs beyond their campus. We will see that we have a unique opportunity to serve not only our graduates, but the ministries, colleagues and communities of our graduates. We will look at a variety of models that have been used to offer both informal and formal training, including that which can be offered by the Internet.

Extension education is not simply reproducing the seminary's courses in locations other than the seminary campus. Developing an extension or distance education program requires the same careful strategic planning process as any other new program that you might chose to begin (chapter 3). Is the potential extension program a reflection of your values and a logical extension of your mission? Are you responding to real needs? Do you have the human and financial resources to be able to do this without hurting your existing training program? Furthermore, extension programs should be built on the same basis as the rest of your curriculum (chapter 6). You need to become aware of what people know and need to know, and then develop a creative and workable plan to get them from here to there.

Distance or Extension Training

Distance education is not a new concept. Correspondence courses were developed by agricultural colleges over 100 years ago. Many universities have both a main campus and extension campuses where the same curriculum is taught. Theological Education by Extension has been widely used since it emerged in Central America in the 1960s. In the last twenty years there has been an explosion of degree programs, professional seminars and practical workshops. For example, MBA programs offered by a variety of British or American universities abound in places like India, South Africa or Eastern Europe. Virtual universities offer web-based training on almost any subject imaginable on a global scale.

The term "distance education" points to the physical separation of instructor and students. As such, correspondence courses or online study are considered distance education. When teachers offer their normal classes off-site as modules, with teacher and students in the same place at the same time, this is called "extended" or "distributed" education.

Nevertheless, the way we actually do education tends to be a fairly complicated mixture. Part-time students take courses both on campus and as part of the "extension" program offered on weekends. Full-time students can do distance education online courses while living on campus and doing traditional courses. It would seem that the distance that matters the most is the relational distance involved in learning. For example, if forty students are enrolled in a university course, most won't interact socially with each other or with the professor before or after class. Perhaps only once in the term will any of them have as much as 15-30 minutes with the teacher in his or her office. Only a handful of extroverts (and largely without much thought) ever comment on much of anything in class.

Web-based interaction, whether done on campus or off campus, can enhance learning. As a teacher assigns readings and questions for reflection, every person is required to respond. As students interact with each other's responses, they get to know each other well. Teachers are also often far more accessible to students by email than in person. Teachers also tend to be more accessible when they lead intensive modules or when they offer weekend courses. As they are together over a period of time with students, relationships are built. Something may be lost by being far away from the library, campus activities or from other students and teachers. Yet something is clearly gained when we teach students in their context and as we use creative less-formal methodologies to reduce the relational distance involved in learning.

There are four basic ways in which we can extend our training programs. We begin by serving our graduates and their colleagues to encourage them in their ministries. We will also extend ourselves as we serve Bible schools and training programs where our graduates work and from which we receive students; as we respond to the needs of the evangelical community around us; and as we offer our curriculum in a variety of ways and locations.

Extending Ourselves by Serving Our Graduates

The greatest impact that any training institution has comes from the relationships that have been developed with its students. Most of us cannot recall many of the words said during our years of school. But we can all remember those who made an impact on us. They shaped who we are and how we minister. We are honored when our teachers continue to write to us, to ask about us or to pray with or for us.

One of the people who did this for me was Dr Herbert Kane, who taught for many years at Trinity Evangelical Divinity School in Chicago. Dr Kane knew much about the church in China and elsewhere. As one of my interests was in churches in communist environments, I did an individual reading course with Dr Kane. I found him to be a wonderful resource person. After he retired from teaching, I discovered that he prayed for me every Tuesday. He rarely wrote, though this godly international scholar actually read and reread my prayer letters before bringing me before God's throne every Tuesday morning. This is part of being a lifelong mentor. I have had several individuals like him who took the initiative to stay in touch with me and with what I do. I treasure these relationships, because I love their advice, encouragement and prayers.

We have the same opportunity with those who come to study with us. Some of the relationships that we build with our students will continue well beyond the time that they spend in our classes. They won't necessarily remember our words any more than we remember the words of our teachers, but they will remember us. We extend the influence of our training programs as we consciously build lifelong relationships with our graduates.

Knowing where and how our graduates are is more than fodder for good public relations, although the success of our graduates is probably the best illustration of why it is worth investing in what we are doing. A student at the Alliance Biblical Seminary in the Philippines once commented to me, "I'm working in a shanty town area, and so far we have managed to plant seven churches." Wow! The ministry of the seminary was not to plant churches in shantytowns, but it *was* to equip those who do! We should discover and share the stories of what God is doing through our students.

As a way of learning more about a seminary that I visited in Zambia, I asked its principal to tell me about their graduates. He looked up at the ceiling and proceeded to tell me from memory about every one of their seventy-three graduates, where they were and how they were. He cared about them and worked at staying in touch. It wasn't surprising to learn that the school had developed a variety of activities every year to reach out to these graduates.

How can we encourage our graduates and their ministries? We can imitate the Apostle Paul who kept in touch with his churches by occasionally visiting them, writing to them and praying for them. Perhaps this feels like something beyond the "call of duty" for our very busy teachers. Fair enough. But if you want to extend your program's influence, you will need to give your teachers both time and a mandate to stay in touch with their students. Much of this can be done via email, though it is also good to occasionally visit them. I was recently with the director of a missions training institution in South Africa. He visits every one of their graduates in their field of service at least once every two years. While he is with them, he also facilitates bringing them together within their region for short refresher courses.

It can also be good to find ways to have them visit you. Our encouragement for our graduates should include offering them something that we are good at: educational training. As you learn about their ongoing needs, you can design seminars or courses to respond to those needs. You could invite all your alumni "home" once a year for refresher courses, or to up-grade them on developments in ministry. Maybe you need to consider developing upper-level training (whether as an entire extension program or as individual modular courses) at the master's or doctoral level to further equip them for the specific issues that they face.

All teachers routinely tell their students in class: "You won't understand this just yet, but the day will come when this will be very important to you." When that day finally arrives, it is good to still be available to them. They also will encounter many situations for which they weren't given any specific training at all. They will turn for help and advice to those who have already been their teachers. Our primary extension program is to be of service to them.

Extending Ourselves by Serving Other Training Institutions

Every seminary is a seminary planting institution. Most of our students are likely to teach in existing Bible schools or to initiate training programs in their churches or areas. Each of these training efforts will functionally be an extension of our program. As our students have been taught in the presence of many witnesses, they now teach those who are also capable of teaching others (2 Tim 2:2). Our students will inevitably replicate what they have learned from us, including the methodologies that we used to teach them.

Through the very difficult years of the 1980s in Ethiopia, the Evangelical Theological College of Addis Ababa functioned essentially as an underground Bible school. After about ten years, they were able to move to a new location under the umbrella of the International Evangelical Church. At the inauguration of new buildings for the church and seminary, they offered a workshop for the various Bible schools in Ethiopia. They discovered that they had become a mother to almost thirty other Bible schools. As their students graduated and began to work in areas where there was no training, many of them started new training programs.

There are two important implications here. The first is a curricular issue. If the vast majority of our graduates are becoming teachers, or are giving leadership to training institutions, we need to prepare them for these roles. As we understand what our graduates need to know and know how to do, we need to include practical teacher training and issues of educational administration in the curriculum. The second implication is related to extension training. We need to recognize that we are in a unique position to influence a phenomenal number of leadership training programs, including many so-called grassroots programs. Responding to this opportunity is an important aspect of how we extend our own training.

That bridges have not been built between various levels of training may be our fault, especially as the pastors to which we have given formal degrees look down on lower-level training or education by extension programs. The only "real" training that they know is what they themselves have experienced. Leaders at so-called "lower-level" programs feel this. I did a workshop in one African country and got the distinct impression that to be assigned to teach at one of their bottom-end programs is perceived as a kind of ecclesiastical punishment. They felt strongly that honor was only given to those who taught in their upper-level institutions.

This is bad thinking. To equip all of God's people for works of service requires a variety of quality training options offered at a variety of levels. We extend our training program and our influence with other training programs by presenting theory about equipping and teaching to our present students, and then involving them experientially in real-life training. We need "barefoot teachers" like the Chinese had during the early years of the Chinese Revolution. University students were sent to rural areas to teach literacy and primary health care. In exposing our students to a variety of teaching situations, our students will gain a vision for training as well as the skills they will need in order to respond to the training needs of the people that they will serve when they graduate. We should help them know how to develop and use training curriculum for local churches and to acquire experience in doing teacher training and program administration. It might also be a good idea to require your faculty to occasionally teach at different levels and in different training settings, lest they lose their own understanding of what is involved in equipping all of God's people for ministry.

It should not be your goal to acquire an educational empire, whereby you functionally run a series of lower-level "extension" schools. Our desire is to encourage quality in training, not to control the many different ways in which training is done. We can assist others by providing short-term teachers, or through offering seminars on teacher training, curriculum development or administration. But partnership with them should not become ownership of them.

It is worth remembering that many of our students may come from these lower-level training programs. We are investing in the quality of our own future students as we work to improve the quality of the training institutions from which they come.

Our influence should extend to theological education by extension programs as well. The best of adult education can be found in good TEE programs where people who are actively involved in ministry meet regularly with a trained facilitator to discuss the integration and application of what they have learned through their study of well-written programmed textbooks. This can be a wonderful way to learn. However, what few good programmed materials exist have mostly been developed by specialists in educational studies and most good study groups are led by foreign-trained experts. After a few years, most TEE teachers tend to become lecturers and not facilitators. There also are few library resources available to help students enrich their understanding of what they are learning. Nobody who graduates from a TEE program knows how to write TEE materials, and TEE curriculum is not normally integrated with any other kind of training.

Theological education by extension is an educational idea worth investing in. Your students (and faculty) need to acquire the skills of teaching by asking questions in order to help students apply materials that they study on their own. You may want to structure some of your in-house classes with TEE-like adult-learning methodologies to help your students appreciate this as an excellent way of learning so that they can teach others as they themselves have been taught. We can also help our students understand the educational philosophy and techniques involved in writing culturally appropriate programmed training materials. One of our extension workshops may be to host people interested in writing these kinds of textbooks. Another extension training seminar that could be offered is on mastering the kinds of facilitation skills that allow TEE to work well. We also may be able to serve a number of lower-level training programs, including TEE, by helping to develop church-based regional study centers with basic working libraries, including (if possible) CD-ROM books and Internet access.

As you hopefully become a mother to many good training programs at a variety of levels, you will want to occasionally bring everyone "home." If you have used good training models, and continue to have regional impact and influence over how theological training is done, your graduates and all those who have benefited from your help will want to participate in your consultations and workshops as you consider important, practical issues related to training.

Extending Ourselves by Serving Churches and the Community

The ministry of theological training institutions should be an extension of the local church. However, we won't satisfy very many felt needs by simply offering courses from our curriculum in local church settings. Good teaching is always context specific. Like every other aspect of curricular design, as we gain a better understanding or profile of those that we are trying to serve in our extension efforts, we will be more effective in offering something that will actually be useful to them. Who are our students? What do they know or know how to do, and what do they need to know or know how to do?

There isn't wisdom in deciding for others what they need. One needs to listen to local churches and Christian leaders to understand what they want as well as to see what they are already doing. It is only as we know something about their needs and realities that we can dialogue intelligently with them about how our resources, expertise and program could serve their churches or organizations.

In chapter 6 we mentioned three schools in Lebanon that rewrote their curriculum based on the entry profile of their students and the desired exit profile of their graduates. Since the discipleship training offered in the first year of this curriculum was useful to any Christian, the courses were taught not only on campus, but also in local churches. They were designed so that they could be offered almost anywhere within the Arabic-speaking world, using correspondence materials or small group facilitators. Visiting teachers in modular seminars or evening courses in local churches could be used as well as semester-long classes at any of the three Bible schools.

Some of the lay leadership development courses of the second year were also offered in churches using local church leadership as teachers. Only the last two years of the BTh program, designed to equip pastors and denominational leadership, were not taught in extension centers, but in the three cooperating schools, using their own teachers or those qualified to teach these subjects at this level.

There are many ways to extend training programs to churches and to the community. This may be as simple as allowing the library to be used by local pastors, or using the school's teachers to offer seminars or workshops that respond to specific felt needs. Conferences or consultations could be held to which local churches and Christian leaders are invited. One seminary that has done this well is SETECA (the Central American Theological Seminary) in Guatemala City, Guatemala. In addition to degree programs that are offered in a variety of creative ways, each Monday, up to 600 pastors come to the school's campus for practical lectures by faculty or invited guests on topics relevant to local ministries. Saturdays focus on different ministries of the church. On one Saturday each month, Sunday school teachers from a variety of denominations meet for master lessons on methodology or background for the materials being taught to children and adults. Other Saturdays are designed for those giving leadership to youth ministries, women's ministries or for those involved in worship and music. SETECA also holds conferences and special weeks of spiritual emphasis each year, events to which the community is always invited.

This is not only scratching where it itches, it is also good public relations. Creatively considering how to extend your program strengthens your relationships with those who consider you to be their school. Their confidence is increased as they hear faculty and students preach and teach. You retain credibility and their ongoing support as they hear your theology, feel your passion and observe your lives. You also will be better able to understand the world of your students and of the needs of the churches as you yourselves minister in that world.

Extending Ourselves Formally

This is what most schools understand as extension studies, though it is important to be aware of how a leadership training institution extends itself as it consciously reaches out to its graduates, to other training institutions and to churches and communities. In formal extension studies, there are a number of ways in which Bible schools and seminaries offer their degree-level programs beyond what is done in a traditional campus-based setting. We will examine seven models of how this can be done.

1. Extension Study Centers

Some schools offer their extension classes in local churches. Trinity Evangelical Divinity School in Chicago offers courses for credit at churches in Wisconsin and Indiana. Other training programs have created whole new campuses, such as Gordon-Conwell Theological Seminary in Massachusetts with extension locations in Charlotte, North Carolina and Orlando, Florida. The Evangelical Theological Seminary in Osijek, Croatia, which for a number of years was the only residential training program in Eastern Europe, offered its courses in key churches located in countries throughout the region. Some training programs offer their degrees on the campuses of other training programs. Dallas Theological Seminary runs a Spanish-language extension of its Doctor of Ministries program through SETECA in Guatemala. Some extension programs have been created for specific needs. For several years the Nairobi Evangelical Graduate School of Theology (NEGST) in Kenya coordinated a long-distance extension of their diploma program for Rwandan refugees in Goma, Zaire. The Biblical Seminary of Colombia in Medellin offers classes for prisoners in a high-security facility. All of these are formal extension studies, courses offered for credit from an administrative home base.

2. Part-time Study for Credit

Most theological training institutions allow students to study part-time, working their way slowly towards a degree. Part-time students occasionally study alongside full-time students in the normal program of study. Alternatively, Bible schools or seminaries offer a week's worth of classes during an entire day, such as on a Monday or a Saturday. Some full-time day programs offer some of their classes in the evening, and open them to the community. Alternatively, in Brazil, where most upper-level training occurs in the evenings, some seminaries also offer occasional day classes. All these extension courses can be taught either on campus or off-site.

3. Intensive Modular Courses

These are often designed for people already involved in full-time ministry, although they can also be used to take advantage of quality visiting lecturers. One single topic will be covered, often during vacation or holiday times. Much of the reading for the course should be done prior to the module so that, like good TEE instruction, class time does not fundamentally need to be used for lectures, but for interaction with an expert who can help with the integration and application of what is being learned. These modules may be offered almost anywhere, including on campus.

4. Degree-level Education by Extension

The TAFTEE network, based in Bangalore, India, has about 7,000 students enrolled at centers throughout India. TAFTEE offers accredited degrees from the certificate through the doctoral level. They have excelled in developing and testing over forty theological texts in several major languages of India. Students study on their own, then meet in groups with one of the nearly 900 people who serve as mentors. The Arabic-language Program for Theological Education by Extension (PTEE), based in Amman, Jordan, uses trained tutors with well-tested materials to offer degree-level training not only in the Middle East and across North Africa, but wherever there are groups of Arabic-speaking Christians wanting to study.

5. Research Centers

Some master's- and doctoral-level training is done as a combination of modular training and individual research. A campus exists with faculty and a library, with students required to spend a week or two each year on campus to work with their mentors and to participate in occasional seminars. Some students opt to spend significant periods of time on campus for personal study, though as the degrees are largely research-based, most students do their work somewhere else, staying in touch with their mentors by email.

Examples of study centers are the Akrofi-Christallar Center in Ghana, the Oxford Centre for Mission Studies in the UK, the Evangelical Theology Faculty in Belgium and Chancellor University in Malawi.

6. *Correspondence or Independent Study*

Few theological training programs will want their entire degree programs to be available by correspondence study, although this is what is done by the University of South Africa (UNISA) in Pretoria, whose 200,000 or so students are guided through their studies by long-distance mentors using print materials. As correspondence study tends to be almost exclusively content-focused, this is a methodology that can be used effectively for courses that require mastering general or foundational truths. Correspondence study has traditionally used printed textbooks, supplemented with videos or cassette tapes. According to an online paper by Doug Valentine of the University of Oklahoma, "China uses a radio and television delivery system to serve 1.5 million students, two-thirds of which are in a degree program."[1] Increasingly, correspondence study is done online via the Internet or with interactive CDs.

Correspondence study can be a good way for some students to reduce the amount of time they need to be on campus. Every curriculum has foundational courses that don't require extensive adaptation to cultural issues or to the specific needs of individual students. These can be developed as independent study courses, though they will not be effective if they are only "talking heads" using videos of class lectures. However, computers have endless patience and can offer drills and practice exercises repeatedly to make sure that students master material well. Courses, complete with exercises, exams and the required readings, can be placed onto CDs for individuals to use wherever they have a computer. Students can also download courses wherever there is access to a high-speed Internet connection. While tech-support needs to be found locally, teachers are readily accessible by email.

A group of students could work through independent study materials together under the guidance of a trained facilitator, as is done with TEE programs. Perhaps a training center for groups of students could be built around computer labs. Research-based seminars can be done under

---

1. Doug Valentine, "Distance Learning: Promises, Problems and Possibilities," *Journal of Distance Learning Administration* 5, no. 3 (Fall 2002): 2.

the guidance of a web-savvy professor bringing together the "threaded" contributions of students working from a variety of locations.

It is not necessary for every training institution to have its own experts to produce independent study materials or electronic courses, as many quality courses have already been developed by others. Adapting or using these courses as part of the general curriculum can be an effective way to offer extension classes for credit. However, administering or teaching Internet-based extension courses is a skill that requires special training. I have listed some resource materials and examples of web-based training courses at the end of this chapter.

Sadly, technology has not made it into most classrooms. Many teachers don't know how to take advantage of computers, video, power point or other electronic resources to enhance what they have always done. Most don't know how to design assignments to help students sort through the good and the bad of the massive amount of information found on the Internet. It is important to help our teaching team know how to incorporate the tools of information technology into all levels of training, including our extension programs.

7. Internet or Virtual Seminaries

Some enthusiastic supporters of electronic learning argue that there isn't a need for thousands of costly seminaries and Bible schools around the world. All that is required is a user-friendly global curriculum for leadership training, using interactive technologies and multimedia, and drawing on some of the world's greatest teachers. Several such training packages already exist. We have noted that electronic tools can enhance the quality of instruction both in traditional classrooms and in extension training programs. However, a virtual seminary, as a complete electronic package of theological training, is built on four questionable assumptions:

1. *That global packages with world-class technology and teachers are better than what can be done locally.* One-size-fits-all solutions are not the best way to train people. That's not a critique of electronic tools, but a belief about the nature of curriculum. Excellence in education starts with real people who are being equipped for real ministries. As teachers get to know their students, they can adapt whatever resources are available to help their students grow.

2. *That character or ministry skills can be developed merely by means of technology.* Generic questions can encourage individual reflection on personal spiritual disciplines, habits or ethical issues. However, putting ideas, convictions and skills into the practice of daily living requires mentors and a community in which a person is held accountable. Furthermore, biblical preaching does not look the same in Singapore, Lusaka or Buenos Aires. To provoke life change needs more than stories and questions, just as mastering ministry skills requires more than video clips of great preachers. Students need supervised hands-on practical experience.

3. *That students (and teachers) are ready and eager to use technology.* There are skills involved in both teaching and learning via the Internet. Although the quality of electronic materials is improving, developing courses for Internet use involves much more than posting class notes and assignments. As those who have tried to teach using the Internet have discovered, teachers and students normally need a fair bit of orientation and ongoing technical assistance for this kind of training to work well.

4. *That equipment exists and that operating costs are affordable.* It may be cheaper to organize a computer lab than a whole new college campus, but by no stretch of the imagination are virtual seminaries cheap. The vast majority of CD courses are not free. Computers are also expensive and wear out quickly in heat, dust and humidity. They require ongoing technical support. Electricity and phone lines may not always be reliable. High-speed Internet may be prohibitively expensive or even inaccessible for many individual learners.

Much has been written about "best practices" in virtual education by those who are using it. Problems are being solved regarding many of the issues mentioned above. Dr Rich Starcher, an educational consultant with the Evangelical Free Church, noted that most of those institutions that deliver quality online courses do so as part of a total program of study (personal email, 5 September 2006). That's good news. Computer labs won't replace classrooms as technology can't replace teachers. Equally, good education requires using a variety of learning methodologies, including technology. Electronic study will enhance our training efforts in many ways, especially as it is integrated into the bigger package of the good things that we are already doing to effectively equip real people for ministry.

Why Extension Education May Fail

1. When it doesn't fit locally. Many extension programs have been developed (and funded) by Westerners who may or may not have done their homework about local needs. A number of extension training efforts died because the courses they offered were simply translated from other contexts or languages with minimal or no field testing.

2. When too much is already there. People who create new programs often seem unaware that any other programs even exist. Alternatively, they see themselves as so unique and superior that they choose not to cooperate with or build on existing training structures or programs. Their efforts focus on creating a market for themselves as a better alternative. This doesn't always work.

3. When there is a lack of local ownership. Without the buy-in from the outset by local churches or Christian organizations, most programs won't work very well.

4. When the costs were not counted. It takes time, energy and funding to properly create and administer any viable program, including electronic ones. A program that works well has probably taken as much time to develop course mentors and a network of facilitators as it gave to course development.

5. When there is a lack of library resources, especially in local languages. Most extension centers do not have even the minimal libraries required for study. This is often an even more critical problem for correspondence or individual study. At the minimum, students need to develop a workable personal library and to learn how to use books (and not just class notes and outlines) for their own continued growth. Acquiring a working library is especially important in a culture where there aren't community libraries and bookshops.

Conclusions

Experience has shown that educational methodologies can be adapted for almost any context. We need to be creative in developing multiple forms and options to extend our programs and influence to our graduates, their churches and the community in general. As we respond to needs, our courses may or may not lead toward degrees. Theological training institutions also have a unique opportunity to serve as resource centers, especially in encouraging and equipping other training programs. Extension training that is excellent will be relational, pragmatic and done in context. However, not all extension efforts will succeed. It is acceptable to try things that might not work. But let us also learn from experience so that our extension efforts will be of service to many others.

Discussion Questions Regarding the Extension of Your Training

1. What are you doing to extend your program and your resources in order to serve your graduates?
2. Make a list of all the Bible schools and seminaries from which you either have received students or in which your graduates are currently serving. How could you help to strengthen these training programs?
3. How might you be able to encourage lower-level training programs, such as TEE or church-based training efforts? Would they be open to your working with them to write or revise their curricular materials? Are there seminars that you could offer to train their teachers or administrators?
4. In what way could you extend your program and your resources to respond to the practical needs of churches and their leaders in the area around you?
5. Which of the formal ways of extending your degree programs have you already tried? With what success? What might you try (or try again), and what would it cost you in time, personnel and finances to make this happen?
6. To what extent have you effectively integrated electronic learning tools into the way that you teach? How can you equip your staff to better take advantage of the many tools that are available?

Websites concerning Electronic Distance Education

http://www.ed.psu.edu/acsde/ – An index by Penn State University listing global organizations working with distance education, as well as materials, periodicals, accreditation, etc.

http://accessweb.org/ – ACCESS (Association of Christian Continuing Education Schools and Seminaries).

http://www.bild.org/ – BILD is a creative organization philosophically committed to develop materials and programs for church-based theological education (C-BTE) globally.

http://www.christiancourses.com (or //cc.christiancourses.com/) Formerly Christian University Global Net. Online learning courses and other digital resources are listed and available through a variety of delivery systems, including Internet, CD-ROM and DVDs.

http://www.teenet.net/ – TEENET is a global network of contextual, community-based, and open theological education to help the indigenous church through formats such as distance education, theological education by extension and diversified learning.

Suggestions for Further Reading

Bates, A. W., and Gary Poole. *Effective Teaching with Technology in Higher Education.* San Francisco, CA: Jossey-Bass, 2003.

Cyrs, Thomas E. "Competence in Teaching at a Distance." *New Direction in Teaching and Learning* 71 (Fall 1997): 15–18.

Derlin, Roberta L., and Edward Erazo. "Distance Learning and the Digital Library: Transforming the Library into an Information Center." *New Directions for Adult and Continuing Education* 71 (Fall 1997).

Dreyfus, Hubert L. "How Far is Distance Learning from Education?" In *On the Internet*, edited by Hubert L. Dreyfus. New York, NY: Routledge, 2001.

Goodson, Carolyn. *Providing Library Services for Distance Education Students.* New York, NY: Neal-Schuman, 2001.

Herrman, Allan, Robert Fax, and Anna Boyd. "Unintended Effects in Using Learning Technologies." *New Directions for Adult and Continuing Education* 88 (Winter 2000): 39–48.

Merriam, Sharan B., and Rosemary S. Caffarella. *Learning in Adulthood: A Comprehensive Guide.* 2nd ed. San Francisco, CA: Jossey-Bass. 1999.

Mood, Terry Ann. *Distance Education: An Annotated Bibliography.* Englewood, CO: Libraries Unlimited, 1995.

Olgren, Christine H. "Learning Strategies for Learning Technologies." *New Directions for Teaching and Learning* 88 (Winter 2000): 7–16.

Palloff, Rena M., and Keith Pratt. *Lessons from the Cyberspace Classroom: The Realities of Online Teaching.* San Francisco, CA: Jossey-Bass, 2001.

Snook, Stewart G. *Developing Leadership through Theological Education by Extension: Case Studies from Africa.* Wheaton, IL: Billy Graham Center, 1992.

"Theological Education by Extension and Technology: A Report on an international consultation held at Vancouver School of Theology," 2–6 June 1997. *Ministerial Formation* (April 1998): 17–26.

Valentine, Doug. "Distance Learning: Promises, Problems and Possibilities." Online *Journal of Distance Learning Administration* 5, no. 3 (Fall 2002).

Western Cooperative for Educational Telecommunications. "Best Practice for Electronically Offered Degree and Certificate Programs." A document developed by eight regional accreditation associations in the US. The document can be found at https://wcet.info/services/publications/ accreditation/ accrediting_bestPractices.pdf#search=%22wiche%20best%20practices%20.

12

Excellence in Evaluation and Renewal

Organizational transformation and renewal is present at each stage in the life of an excellent training institution. Evaluation is structured into the ongoing life of each aspect of the program. Being a part of a broader network and learning from others is an important part of renewal.

The overall value of a good education is not easily quantifiable, nor can it easily be demonstrated which piece of the training program actually contributed to the success of one of our graduates. How can we take credit for what God's Spirit did in our midst? On the other hand, how do we know that we haven't been wasting our time and resources in our educational efforts, especially given that the primary impact of our training comes from the intangibles of our training environment and from relationships?

It often is simpler to show where we have failed than to identify what we've done to succeed, but even in failure it is not always clear what went wrong. A disturbing number of students manage to move through North American public school systems without acquiring even basic skills and knowledge, in some cases, graduating while remaining functionally illiterate. Standardized tests may clearly show that there *is* a problem, but trying to develop solutions is complicated since the reasons for failure can be multiple, including poor curriculum, lousy students, too few teachers, teachers who don't know how to teach, or inadequate facilities.

We can't claim success if our carefully crafted and well-staffed program has been training the wrong people. Neither can we feel successful when our graduates fail in ministry because they weren't trained in the right things. We don't want to become adult day-care centers or scholarship-funded refugee camps, providing free housing, food, medical care and diplomas for people who didn't have anything better to do anyway.

We also cannot affirm our excellence if our invisible curriculum triumphed over whatever else we thought we achieved. A curriculum can be wonderfully contextual, appropriately accredited and with students who demonstrate their brilliance on every standardized test, but we have not done well if we produce an arrogant elite rather than godly Christian leaders who work as servants in a community. Neither have we succeeded if one of the outcomes of our efforts has been to contribute to the unnecessary multiplication of training options as each of our graduates starts his or her own new school rather than encouraging the quality of existing training efforts within the region.

In this chapter we want to look at issues of renewal and evaluation. How can the impact of a training institution be discerned in order to make it more effective? How can faculty and administrative teams be renewed? And how can we become a learning community that renews itself?

Is It Worth the Time and Expense?

There's a lot that isn't perfect in what we do. Students will not remember most of what was said in class. Not all of them will do well in ministry. The lives of faculty are not always consistent illustrations of what they teach. Misunderstandings occur in the educational community. The content of every subject could be more up-to-date. Classes could be better organized and taught with better pedagogy.

Evaluation and renewal have been themes throughout this book. We affirm again that excellence does not mean perfection. But for us to assess our excellence requires us to review what we intended to do. For those who haven't aimed at anything specific, there is no way of affirming what was or was not accomplished.

Evaluation is an essential part of every strategic plan. Were our values and purpose visible in what we did? Did we use the resources we had to adequately respond to needs around us? How have we seen God use us and our efforts to equip the students that we had for the ministries to which he called them? In the light of our intended outcomes we can examine our practices, processes, people and results in order to understand the extent to which we have achieved what we intended.

The truth is, you may be too tired to see what God has done, and continues to do, through you. Corporate and individual renewal must be part of an evaluation process. I listened to an academic dean present a workshop about the difficulty of trying to provoke change in her institution. I sensed discouragement as she talked. There is always a long list of things needing improvement. However, the point of evaluation is not to be overwhelmed by things needing attention or all the mountains yet to be climbed. Her institution is one the finest programs I know. Before feeling frustration over what yet needs to be done, they needed to remember how God has blessed them and used them.

Perhaps this feels like an exercise in giving "thanks in all circumstances" (1 Thess 5:18). But even in the midst of huge messes, we need to remember that God has been at work, and that his lifelong curriculum will not fail. We have never been more than one piece of what God is doing in the lives of our students. We do God an injustice if we make too much of what "we" have failed to do. Evaluation must begin by looking for the hand of God in our midst.

This doesn't negate our need to look carefully at our track record in the light of our mission and objectives. We don't have the luxury of sitting on our laurels as we simply perpetuate the past. It takes courage and effort to build on the past in order to continue to be in a position to be used by God in the lives of our students.

Organizational Life Cycles

Schools, like people and organizations, have life cycles. Schools often come into existence through the enthusiasm and tireless efforts of a visionary founder. In its early years, a training program runs on very limited resources, although everyone happily pitches in with teaching and administrative tasks. As a school moves towards maturity, it becomes stable and respectable. The academic program is properly accredited with a well-crafted curriculum taught by qualified specialists. As an established program, proper administrative departments are competently led. There is a healthy student body, a great governing board and adequate finances to maintain the institution forever.

To some extent, evaluation will be different for a brand new program than for one that has been around for a while. For younger programs, the biggest need is usually for consolidation to bring order and organization to the many new things being done. An older program has a greater need to make sure that it is not being lulled to sleep by its own traditions. Nevertheless, one awkward question needs to be asked of all programs. Should "death" also be a part of an organizational life cycle?

Admittedly lots of training programs cease to exist, usually for very sad reasons. Perhaps there never were enough students or funding, or maybe the institution slowly faded away to the point where it was no longer viable. Maybe a major conflict or a scandal destroyed it. Training institutions can die. But should they? Is this a part of a normal life cycle for a theological program?

One of the more important questions in an evaluation is to determine whether there still is a task for you to do or whether you have finished what God asked of you. One shouldn't perpetuate that which is no longer needed. Neither should you continue with something that is only marginally viable. Perhaps it would be better to join together with another like-minded training ministry. I have heard it said that the average Bible school in Africa has only ten students. If this is true, it is not surprising that many programs struggle. As you reconsider what you are and could be, remember that these are viable strategic options: merging with others, or finding a gracious way to quit. Why carry on if we are not convinced that what we are doing is worth the effort?

The Renewal of Your Training

This book has been written to help you assess your institutional excellence. The process for doing an evaluation was outlined in chapter 3 as we looked at strategic planning. Four big questions need to be asked:

1. What should be affirmed and strengthened?
2. What is weak and needs to be fixed?
3. What is weak and should be dropped altogether?
4. What are we not doing that should be started?

Evaluation is not an activity to be done by a committee every five to ten years in preparation for re-accreditation. It should be an ongoing process of being aware of what God is doing in our midst and discovering how we can better pursue excellence in training leaders to the glory of God.

The way to begin an evaluation is with a party. Without glossing over the problems that everyone may be aware of, find specific ways that God has used you and blessed you. Gather feedback from a variety of directions. We may not be able to see much progress within the day-to-day grind of the educational process. The real impact is seen in the product, which is often only visible in the life and ministry of a student well after he or she graduates. Find ways to listen to your graduates individually and collectively as they reflect on the value of the training you gave them. Listen also to how those churches and Christian organizations that have received your graduates feel about them.

Then rejoice and celebrate the goodness of God. Affirm all that is good and creatively consider how it can be strengthened. If there is nothing to celebrate, the time has come to close up shop altogether. However, it is almost inconceivable that you won't be able to uncover a long list of wonderful things that have happened.

As we discussed in chapter 3 ("Excellence in Strategic Planning") each piece of a training institution can and should be evaluated. One good way to systematically do this is through the self-study review that is part of an accreditation or re-accreditation process. This provides a series of questions based on standards of practice that are internationally acknowledged as indicators of quality in the training of leaders for ministry and the church. Working through the questions and documenting the extent to which these standards are being met is a good way to work towards institutional excellence as well as to review and affirm the excellence that already exists. Many schools say that working through the self-evaluation review has been one of the best things that they have done to help them understand their strengths and weaknesses.

The additional advantage of working with an accreditation agency is that someone will read through your self-evaluation report carefully and give written feedback to the school. When both the school and the accrediting agency feel that the institution is ready for an accreditation visit, a team will come to verify that what the school feels about itself is true. This kind of external evaluation is a helpful affirmation of your internal evaluation and also includes a written report of commendations and recommendations.

Most governments also want to verify that training programs within their countries satisfactorily meet the minimum required standards for education. You will again be doing evaluation as you prepare and provide the massive documentation that these authorities need, and you should once again benefit by the visit and report of their external evaluation team.

However, as we noted in chapter 4 ("Excellence in Governance"), the most significant evaluation and affirmation of our training efforts will come from those who are the beneficiaries of what we are doing, especially our graduates and the churches and Christian organizations they serve. Later in this chapter we will discuss further how to become a learning community in order to obtain the kind of feedback that will constantly help us know what is good and should continue, what is weak and needs strengthening, what should be dropped altogether as it no longer is needed and what needs to be added to make our training programs even better.

The Renewal of Your People: Why?

One of the *Seven Laws of the Learner* is the Law of Revival.[1] Wilkinson states: "Realize that revival is needed by most Christians most of the time."[2] There are lots of reasons why leaders, teachers and all of our administrative and academic staff can become discouraged or just plain worn out.

- **Self-sacrifice.** Everyone needs to carry his or her cross and to deny personal desires in order to follow the Lord. There are many things less stressful than taking on the responsibilities and burdens of being a leader or a teacher. The cost of discipleship is high.

- **Loneliness**. Elijah complained to the Lord, "I have had enough!" (1 Kgs 19:4). He continued, "I have been very zealous for the Lord God Almighty. The Israelites have rejected your covenant, broken down your altars, and put your prophets to death with the sword. I am the only one left, and now they are trying to kill me too" (1 Kgs 19:10). Although it wasn't true that he was the only one, he certainly felt that way. God had used him to do incredible things,

---

1. Bruce Wilkinson, *Seven Laws of the Learner* (Atlanta, GA: Walk-Thru-The Bible, 1990).
2. Ibid., 381.

yet now Elijah was discouraged and fleeing for his life from Queen Jezebel. Many of those involved in training have also been greatly used by God. But people can feel so alone or so tired that they become discouraged and want to give up.

- **Criticisms, rejection and enemies**. Moses was initially received with enthusiasm by the people he had been sent to liberate, although they soon turned against him as Pharaoh made life difficult. No amount of miracles really convinced Pharaoh to change. Neither did the people remember God's mighty acts from day to day. They made a golden calf, and whined about food and water. Some of the leaders questioned whether Moses really was the only one holy enough to speak to God. His own brother and sister challenged his leadership. All educational leaders live in an environment where their every action (and that of their families) is critiqued. Jealousies can abound with little room for grace. People don't remember good things for very long, and the slightest error of judgment becoming a rallying point to force a person out.

- **Weariness**. Moses complained to the Lord, "Why have you brought this trouble on your servant? What have I done to displease you that you put the burden of all these people on me? . . . I cannot carry all these people by myself; the burden is too heavy for me. If this is how you are going to treat me, put me to death right now" (Num 11:11, 14–15). It would not have been fun to lead the Israelites through the desert. There was too much to do, and the people were difficult to work with. It was simply "too heavy a burden." That's true of most training institutions as well. There's always too much to do. There often are difficult people with whom to work. There may be few visible results. People reach the end of their emotional and physical energy.

- **Pressure and confusion**. Most people, like Moses, encounter situations where they are not sure what is the best thing to do. Moses actually suggested to the Lord that it would be better for him to die. We may feel equally discouraged as we try to accomplish what feels impossible. Not only are there few available financial or human resources to solve the many problems before us, but we may be working in an environment of strong personalities with major conflicts over values, ideas or programs.

- **Lack of challenge**. Peter Drucker says that "Burnout, much of the time, is a cop-out for being bored."³ Sometimes leadership or ministry becomes little more than maintenance. We feel that nothing has ever changed, and nothing ever will. No one wants to try new things, and no new ideas are even offered. Routine becomes boredom.

- **The pressure of temptations and failure**. Big egos often grow on those in charge of things. Positions of leadership foster personal ambition and encourage a desire to be served rather than serving others. Leaders and teachers can come to love the perks and status that go with their jobs. Those who are honest know their own mixed motives. Yet we often give ourselves so little room for grace. Although the Scriptures remind us that "All have sinned and come short of the glory of God" (Rom 3:23), any failing in ministry is often considered permanently fatal to future ministry. Even though many leaders in Scripture had major failings, people today don't want flaws in their leaders. This does not contribute to transparency or to the possibility of renewal and restoration. The pressure is to appear better than what may be reality. Rather than grow towards healthy maturity, people simply move away permanently.

The Renewal of Your People: How?

- **We are renewed through vision**. Renewal begins with a reaffirmation of what we are all about in our common vision and purpose. Teachers and the administrative staff team should be encouraged as they see the importance that their ministry has for the good of the kingdom because of what they are doing together in equipping students. Everyone needs to be constantly reminded where they are going and how they fit together into helping the institution train students for the ministries that God has for them. People are reaffirmed and renewed as they see and feel their importance within the training process.

- **We are renewed as we work together in teams**. It should be renewing to discover and celebrate the abilities and experience of the people God has

---

3. Peter Drucker, *Managing the Non-Profit Organization* (New York, NY: Harper Business, 1990), 197.

brought together. It is worth listening to the stories about those that God has uniquely equipped to be our colleagues. That we are now together as a team is a complex story that God has woven. While traveling in the Philippines, I met a new faculty member at a training institution located there. She came from a Chinese background and had huge dreams for the school and the entire region built on her experiences and training. As I listened to some of what mattered to her, I thought "What a neat person to have as part of one's faculty team."

I felt that way about Overseas Council's team when I came to work there. People had competence, initiative and creativity as they made a good organization even better. It touched me one day when one of our younger staff members brushed tears from her eyes as she watched a video about what God was doing around the world. One of my favorite people didn't go a week without bringing in yet another huge idea that could impact the entire evangelical world. I found joy in working with these people. They renewed me and hopefully made me more effective in what I did.

- **We are renewed as our skills are renewed**. How can we become better teachers or administrators? How can we use our differing gifts to serve each other better? As we discussed in chapter 7 ("Excellence in Teachers"), renewing our skills involves investing in both formal and informal continuing education. We also will be challenged to change as a result of the evaluations that should be done for every subject taught. We can be renewed through attending conferences, workshops or faculty and staff retreats that focus on specific areas of teaching or administration. Our job description should require reading and research into new things. Informal times of creative interaction should be encouraged. Our whole training program will be renewed as we all learn to do better what we have been called to do.

- **We are renewed by rest**. People will be renewed daily, providing that they are not constantly pushed to exhaustion. No one should be asked to do more than can realistically be expected from him or her. It is not healthy to live from crisis to crisis twenty-four hours a day. As Elijah was fleeing for his life from Jezebel, his renewal began with some extended time for sleeping, accompanied with proper food. He then went away for forty days to meet with God. We all need regular breaks. The concept of Sabbath rest was not given for everyone except those in ministry. Your educational team should be forced to take regular vacations and to enjoy a day off each week. Providing for a sabbatical year can even be career-saving.

- **We are renewed when we are cared for**. Everyone will do their jobs better if their families are adequately cared for. That requires housing, medical coverage and a decent salary. But people also do their jobs better if they live in healthy communities where people care for one another and pray for one another, both privately and publicly.

Becoming a Learning Community

Renewal happens best when there is an educational culture that cares about how things are going. From top to bottom, everyone should be looking for ways to affirm that which is good and to fix that which is struggling. Such an environment is healthier and more satisfying to work in than one where there is constant criticism and fear of failure. As a community, we all need to look for ways to celebrate what God is doing, and not be quick to critique everyone and everything that is not as perfect as we might like it to be.

We do this by becoming a learning community. We need to become listeners to a broad network that regularly provides good feedback. Some of this can be formal feedback, such as the written conclusions of the visitation team verifying your self-evaluation accreditation review or the compilation of the written evaluations done by students after each class subject. We may choose to invite an outside consultant to formally help us evaluate our program and our plans for the future. We also provide formal feedback to individuals through annual performance reviews based on their job descriptions.

However, becoming a learning community fundamentally involves finding informal ways to listen to each other, to alumni, to those key church leaders who are our owners, to our advisory council and governing board, to churches and Christian organizations, and to the community and world in which we serve. We need to find multiple ways by which we can understand more about the impact we have (or don't have) as a training institution.

Feedback isn't primarily about hearing criticism, though learning about failures and receiving suggestions for improvement are important parts of what we need to hear. But everyone should also be encouraged to celebrate with us what God has done in and through our efforts. We should invite everyone we can to dream and pray with us about things that could be done. This kind of feedback doesn't just happen by itself. In order to discern what we are doing well, and to understand what needs to be changed, dropped or added, we may need to convene groups of key pastors, alumni or students. As our faculty and administrative leadership travel, asking for honest feedback should be part of what everyone does. Time should regularly be scheduled into staff, faculty and student meetings for reflection on what and how we are doing. Giving feedback is one of the primary functions of our advisory council and governing board.

There are specific things that we should be learning from different groups.

Learning from Our Graduates

We need to visit our graduates where they are as well as to encourage them to occasionally come back to campus. More than anyone else, they know the totality of our training program and have first-hand experience as to its practical impact. We need to hear their concerns and suggestions. Specifically, we should ask them:
- Of all the courses they took, which ones were the most useful in preparing them for life and ministry?
- Which ones were of the least value and why?
- What do they wish that they had learned or studied, but didn't? How could we do a better job of helping others learn these things?

Learning from the Leaders of Churches or Christian Organizations That Sent Us Their Students

As these people are our "owners" we need to hear their compliments, complaints and suggestions about who we are and what we are doing. There are two basic things that we need to learn from them:
- To what extent do they feel that our graduates returned well-prepared and equipped for the real needs of ministry? Can they preach, do administration, deal with issues of spiritual warfare, develop evangelistic outreaches, do pastoral visits and counseling, teach Bible classes, disciple new believers or provide vision for the church?

- What kind of people were they when they returned? Servants? Team players? Arrogant? Compassionate? Willing to work hard in behind-the-scenes ministry? Scholars more than pastors? Mentors to potential new leaders?

Learning from Students about Their Teachers

We primarily learn from students as part of an evaluation that should be done at the end of every class subject offered. Teachers should not see what individual students write about them. However, a summary should be given to the teacher, ideally as part of a discussion with the academic dean about how the class could be improved. A copy of this summary should also be kept in the personnel file for that teacher. Input from the students is useful in these areas:

- **Personality and attitudes**. Was there humility, respect for the students, awareness of student needs and availability to them, emotional equilibrium, enthusiasm, dedication and openness to criticism?
- **Preparation and teaching competence**. Did the teacher thoroughly understand the subject matter, adequately cover the material, and come prepared and on time, grade fairly and return assignments in a reasonable time?
- **Teaching methodology**. Were ideas presented clearly, the important things emphasized, time used well, a variety of teaching techniques used, and interaction encouraged? Was a healthy group dynamic promoted and learning stimulated?

Learning from Students about the Class Subjects

Three open-ended questions are useful for any class subject:
- What part of the course helped them the most?
- What part of the course was the least important to them?
- What suggestions would they make for improving the course?

Students may love a class that didn't need to be in the curriculum, but which was brilliantly taught. Alternatively, an important subject that was poorly taught may be given low marks from students. An evaluation should have questions that allow us to discern the perceived importance that students

place on the subject itself and not just on how it was taught. There are three primary issues of concern:
- Did the course achieve its goals and objectives? Do these goals and objectives seem to fit in well with other courses being taught?
- Did it respond to the realities of the church or society, and did it give students the knowledge, skills and character needed for serving in the church or elsewhere?
- Was the course designed well? (Balance of how the material is organized, too much or too little material to be covered in one term, or readings and assignments that are appropriate)

Learning from the Teachers about Students

It is good each year for teachers to take time to talk with each other about the students and to pray together for them. Are there any special problem people or issues that need attention? Are these students worth celebrating over? What needs to be done to strengthen the student body? This should not become an opportunity for sharing community gossip. But someone may have noticed something that is more than an idiosyncrasy. I remember a faculty meeting where a teacher raised the issue of a student who routinely came to class barefoot. No one imagined that the student was likely to graduate to become a barefoot pastor, but was there an attitude that needed attention so that the student would not create problems for himself in ministry?

Learning from Teachers about Themselves

Teachers can be given a self-evaluation form to allow them to reflect on themselves and their colleagues. What they write is confidential, although this could be discussed with the academic dean, or become part of a faculty meeting. This can include such questions as:
- How do my subjects relate to the rest of the curriculum?
- What more do I need to know in order to teach my classes more effectively?
- How can I become more creative in my teaching methodologies?
- How are my relationships with colleagues, students and the administration?
- What would strengthen the teaching team that I am a part of?

Learning from Everyone about the Overall Program

We need informal forums during the year not only to celebrate, but to listen to problems before they become crises. Are there issues with the physical facilities, including problems of security, space, lighting or acoustics? Are there problems with specific rules and regulations? Are there unresolved tensions?

Conclusions

May you be renewed as you evaluate what you have been doing, celebrate what God is doing and prayerfully dream about what you could become. Think realistically about what needs to be kept, fixed, dropped or added. Your strategic plan cannot simply be a wish list reflecting the creative enthusiasm of some of your staff, but it should be a carefully prayed-through plan, with adequate funding for the facilities, programs and a faculty and administrative team to equip real students for the ministries that God has for them. I trust that your constituency and owners will delight in you as they benefit from the fruits of what you are doing. May many see your excellence and give praise to God because of you.

Discussions Questions Regarding Your Evaluation and Renewal

1. What is worth celebrating in your program? How do you answer those who may question whether what you are doing is worth the effort, time and expense?
2. Where are you in the organizational life cycle? As you evaluate your institution, what is your biggest need?
3. To what extent are you and your administrative staff and teaching team too weary to do an effective evaluation of yourselves? Why are you or they so worn out? What can be done to renew your team?
4. Are you a learning community? How can you improve the way you receive and use feedback? From whom do you need to do more learning?

Suggestions for Further Reading

Daft, Richard L. *Organizational Theory and Design*. St. Paul, MN: West Publishing, 1992.

Gerig, Donald. "Are We Overworked?" *Leadership* (Summer 1986): 22–25.

MacPhail-Wilcox, Bettye, and Roy Forbes. *Administrator Evaluation Handbook: How to Design a System of Administrative Evaluation*. Bloomington, IN: Phi Delta Kappa, 1990.

Maslach, Christina, and Michael P. Leiter. *The Truth about Burnout*. San Francisco, CA: Jossey-Bass, 1997.

Rudnitsky, Posner. "Planning a Course Evaluation," Chapter 8 in *Curriculum Design*. New York, NY: Longman, s.d.

Simon, Judith Sharken. *5 Life Stages of Nonprofit Organizations*. Saint Paul, MN: Wilder Foundation, 2001.

Vella, Jane. *How Do They Know That They Know?* San Francsico, CA: Jossey-Bass, 1998.

Wilkinson, Bruce H. *The 7 Laws of the Learner*. Portland, OR: Multnomah Press, 1992.

ICETE is a global community, sponsored by nine regional networks of theological schools, to enable international interaction and collaboration among all those engaged in strengthening and developing evangelical theological education and Christian leadership development worldwide.

The purpose of ICETE is:
1. To promote the enhancement of evangelical theological education worldwide.
2. To serve as a forum for interaction, partnership and collaboration among those involved in evangelical theological education and leadership development, for mutual assistance, stimulation and enrichment.
3. To provide networking and support services for regional associations of evangelical theological schools worldwide.
4. To facilitate among these bodies the advancement of their services to evangelical theological education within their regions.

Sponsoring associations include:

Africa: Association for Christian Theological Education in Africa (ACTEA)

Asia: Asia Theological Association (ATA)

Caribbean: Caribbean Evangelical Theological Association (CETA)

Europe: European Evangelical Accrediting Association (EEAA)

Euro-Asia: Euro-Asian Accrediting Association (E-AAA)

Latin America: Association for Evangelical Theological Education in Latin America (AETAL)

Middle East and North Africa: Middle East Association for Theological Education (MEATE)

North America: Association for Biblical Higher Education (ABHE)

South Pacific: South Pacific Association of Evangelical Colleges (SPAEC)

www.icete-edu.org

Langham Literature and its imprints are a ministry of Langham Partnership.

Langham Partnership is a global fellowship working in pursuit of the vision God entrusted to its founder John Stott –

> *to facilitate the growth of the church in maturity and Christ-likeness through raising the standards of biblical preaching and teaching.*

Our vision is to see churches in the majority world equipped for mission and growing to maturity in Christ through the ministry of pastors and leaders who believe, teach and live by the Word of God.

Our mission is to strengthen the ministry of the Word of God through:
- nurturing national movements for biblical preaching
- fostering the creation and distribution of evangelical literature
- enhancing evangelical theological education

especially in countries where churches are under-resourced.

Our ministry

Langham Preaching partners with national leaders to nurture indigenous biblical preaching movements for pastors and lay preachers all around the world. With the support of a team of trainers from many countries, a multi-level programme of seminars provides practical training, and is followed by a programme for training local facilitators. Local preachers' groups and national and regional networks ensure continuity and ongoing development, seeking to build vigorous movements committed to Bible exposition.

Langham Literature provides majority world preachers, scholars and seminary libraries with evangelical books and electronic resources through publishing and distribution, grants and discounts. The programme also fosters the creation of indigenous evangelical books in many languages, through writer's grants, strengthening local evangelical publishing houses, and investment in major regional literature projects, such as one volume Bible commentaries like *The Africa Bible Commentary* and *The South Asia Bible Commentary*.

Langham Scholars provides financial support for evangelical doctoral students from the majority world so that, when they return home, they may train pastors and other Christian leaders with sound, biblical and theological teaching. This programme equips those who equip others. Langham Scholars also works in partnership with majority world seminaries in strengthening evangelical theological education. A growing number of Langham Scholars study in high quality doctoral programmes in the majority world itself. As well as teaching the next generation of pastors, graduated Langham Scholars exercise significant influence through their writing and leadership.

To learn more about Langham Partnership and the work we do visit **langham.org**

www.ingramcontent.com/pod-product-compliance
Lightning Source LLC
Chambersburg PA
CBHW070612170426
43200CB00012B/2661